Season 3

The Way of the Chosen

Amanda Jenkins, Dallas Jenkins, & Douglas S. Huffman

DAVID C COOK

transforming lives together

THE WAY OF THE CHOSEN
Published by David C Cook
4050 Lee Vance Drive
Colorado Springs, CO 80918 U.S.A.

Integrity Music Limited, a Division of David C Cook
Brighton, East Sussex BN1 2RE, England

The graphic circle C logo is a registered trademark of David C Cook.

ISBN 978-0-8307-8456-1
eISBN 978-0-8307-8457-8

The Team: Michael Covington, Stephanie Bennett, Jack Campbell, Susan Murdock
Cover Design: James Hershberger
Introduction and Conclusion Illustration Art: Juicebox Designs

Printed in the United States of America
First Edition 2023

1 2 3 4 5 6 7 8 9 10

100322-LSC

CONTENTS

"Enter by the narrow gate. For the gate is wide and the way is easy that leads to destruction, and those who enter by it are many. For the gate is narrow and the way is hard that leads to life, and those who find it are few."

Matthew 7:13-14

Introduction

THE WAY OF THE CHOSEN

Destruction.

That's a big and terrible word, not to mention an unconventional one to start a Bible study with. But let's just get after it, because we're living in a world of brokenness and woe. Matthew wasn't being prophetic when he used the word; he wasn't making a claim that remained to be seen.

We see it, Matthew.

Truth is, devastation and ruin are around us all the time—just turn on the news. Or any reality TV show. Take a drive and you'll inevitably see bars on windows, trash in gutters, graffiti on walls, and people living in the midst of it on the street. Google the current numbers on divorce, single-parent births, high school dropouts, crime, mental illness, or suicide.

They're all on the rise.

Scan the horizon of your neighborhood, or closer still, take an honest look inside your own life—your friends, your family, *yourself*—and you'll see a thousand different ways the wide road has led to destruction.

And it started all the way back in the Garden of Eden.

Genesis 2:8–3:13

"The LORD God planted a garden in Eden,

in the east, and there he put the man whom

he had formed. And out of the ground the

LORD God made to spring up every tree that

is pleasant to the sight and good for food.

 the tree of life

was in the midst of the garden, and the

tree of the knowledge of good and evil.

a river

flowed out of Eden to water the garden,

and there it divided and became four rivers…. [And] the LORD God

took the man and put him in the garden of Eden to work it and keep it.

And the LORD God commanded the man, saying, 'You may surely eat

of every tree of the garden, but of the tree of the knowledge of good and

evil you shall not eat, for in the day that you eat of it you shall surely die.'

Then the LORD God said, 'It is not good that the man should be alone; I will make him a helper fit for him.' Now out of the ground the LORD God had formed every beast of the field and every bird of the heavens and brought them to the man to see what he would call them. And whatever the man called every living creature, that was its name. The man gave names to all livestock and to

the birds of the heavens

and to every beast of the field.

But for Adam there was not found a helper fit for him. So the LORD God caused a deep sleep to fall upon the man, and while he slept took one of his ribs and closed up its place with flesh. And the rib that the LORD God had taken from the man he made into a woman and brought her to the man....

Now the *Serpent* was more crafty

than any other beast of the field that the LORD God had made.

He said to the woman, 'Did God actually say, "You shall not eat

of any tree in the garden"?' And the woman said to the serpent,

'We may eat of the fruit of the trees in the garden, but God said,

"You shall not eat of the fruit of the tree that is in the midst

of the garden, neither shall you touch it, lest you die."'

But the serpent said to the woman, 'You will not

surely die. For God knows that when you eat of it

your eyes will be opened, and you will be like God,

knowing good and evil.' So when the woman saw

that the tree was good for food, and that it was

a delight to the eyes, and that the tree was to be

desired to make one wise, she took of its fruit and

ate, and she also gave some to her husband who

was with her, and he ate. Then the eyes of both

were opened, and they knew that they were naked.

And they sewed *fig leaves*

together and made themselves loincloths.

And they heard the sound of the LORD God walking in the garden in the *cool of the day*

and the man and his wife hid themselves from the presence of the LORD God among the trees of the garden. But the LORD God called to the man and said to him, 'Where are you?' And he said, 'I heard the sound of you in the garden, and I was afraid, because I was naked, and I hid myself.'

He said, 'Who told you that you were naked? Have you eaten of the tree of which I commanded you not to eat?' The man said, 'The woman whom you gave to be with me, she gave me

fruit of the tree

and I ate.' Then the LORD God said to the woman, 'What is this that you have done?' The woman said, 'The serpent deceived me, and I ate.'"

Tragically, Adam and Eve messed up God's perfect creation. At the very first fork, they chose the wide road and destroyed what God had made, putting distance between them and the Lord and enmity between themselves and the world.

And we're just like them.

We're prone to wander away from God, but we don't have to, and self-sabotage is not a foregone conclusion. There's a different way to live for those who believe Jesus when He says, "I am the way, and the truth, and the life. No one comes to the Father except through me" (John 14:6).

Jesus is the narrow gate that leads to life, but according to the Bible, those who find Him are few. How can that be? Why don't all the ways we've messed up apart from Jesus cause us to run right to Him and to stay there?

The answer is obvious. His way is hard.

By its very nature, following requires submission—which is perhaps one of the most despised words of the twenty-first century. To submit means to yield our desires to someone else. To make personal sacrifices. To exercise self-control and self-denial. To be humble and, oftentimes, to repent. To change our hearts and our very lives when it's required, because submitting means we obey the One who knows better than we do; the One whose ways are different from our own.

> "'For my thoughts are not your thoughts, neither are your ways my ways,' declares the LORD. 'As the heavens are higher than the earth, so are my ways higher than your ways and my thoughts than your thoughts.'"
> Isaiah 55:8–9 NIV

No wonder we so often refuse it and go our own way. But since the consequence of the wide road is our own demise, perhaps it's time to embrace the hard stuff of following and storm the narrow gate.

Perhaps it's time to go the way of the Chosen.

"For if you forgive others their trespasses, your heavenly Father will also forgive you, but if you do not forgive others their trespasses, neither will your Father forgive your trespasses."

Matthew 6:14–15

Lesson 1

FORGIVE
as Jesus forgives

JOHN THE BAPTIST: What did you think of Him?

JOANNA: I don't know how to describe it.

JOHN THE BAPTIST: Like you were grateful for food but didn't realize you'd been starving.

JOANNA: That works.

JOHN THE BAPTIST (*smiling at Andrew*): Anything new?

ANDREW: So much.

JOHN THE BAPTIST: Tell me what He said.

JOANNA: Nothing that made sense. (*John likes where this is going.*)

JOANNA (CONT'D): Everything upside down—the poor, the grieving, the meek, all elevated.

JOHN THE BAPTIST: Blessed.

JOANNA: Yes. And other things reversed ... love your enemies. Who can LOVE their enemy?

JOHN THE BAPTIST: He can. What else?

JOANNA: Bizarre imagery. Something about pearls before pigs, logs in eyes ...

JOHN THE BAPTIST: Yes.

ANDREW: Salt, murder, rain, God feeding the birds, houses on sand.

JOANNA: He's almost as strange as you.

JOHN THE BAPTIST: I wish I were so strange. *(John paces now, excited.)* How many people were there?

JOANNA: Thousands.

JOHN THE BAPTIST: Wonderful. What else?

ANDREW: John … what do we do about you? How can I help?

JOHN THE BAPTIST: You're helping me with what you're sharing.

ANDREW: You know what I mean.

JOHN THE BAPTIST: Come here. *(Andrew leans in.)*

JOHN THE BAPTIST (CONT'D): Don't be afraid. *(Andrew inhales. He is afraid.)*

JOHN THE BAPTIST (CONT'D): The prophecies of Isaiah … He has been sent to proclaim liberty to the captives, and what?

ANDREW: The opening of the prison to those who are bound.

JOHN THE BAPTIST: This prison is nothing now that He's here. Do you believe that?

ANDREW: I'm trying.

JOHN THE BAPTIST: Andrew … in all He said to those thousands of people, there was something just for you. For what you're going through. There always is. What was it? Something that stuck with you.

ANDREW *(pausing, emotional)*: Don't be anxious. Can you add a single hour to your life by being anxious?

JOHN THE BAPTIST: That sounds like Him. What else?

ANDREW: But seek first the kingdom of God and His righteousness.

JOHN THE BAPTIST: Even more like Him. So if you want to help me … Andrew? *(Andrew looks up.)* If you want to help me … listen to Him. Go home and do what He says. That's what I want. Got it?

Upside Down

If you're all caught up on *The Chosen*, you know season 2 closed with Jesus beginning to preach His most famous sermon. That landmark message has come to be known as the "Sermon on the Mount" (or SOM, for short)—which is exactly where season 3 picks up. But the focus of episode 1 isn't merely on Jesus's teaching. It's also on the way His followers understand His words and apply them to the complexities of their lives.

And that's *always* the hard part, right? Jesus's words sound great and inspiring and true until the rubber meets the road and we have to actually apply them, starting with one of the most impossible exhortations of all: forgive others their trespasses.

Truth is, following Jesus often entails seeing and doing things that are opposite our instincts. As Joanna put it, a lot of what Jesus said seems upside down to us; nothing makes sense. Things like the first will be last and the last will be first (Matt. 19:30), to lead we must serve (Matt. 23:11), to gain we must give (Luke 6:38), to live we must die (Mark 8:35), and to inherit the world we must first become poor, meek, and peace-seeking even in the face of persecution (Matt. 5:2–10).

Not exactly a wooing message in our "me first" world.

That is, unless every other road leads to destruction.

Your Turn

1. What does "the first will be last and the last will be first" mean in the context of Matthew 19:16–30? In what ways are you living that principle? In what ways are you not?

For Bible Nerds (like us) Who Want to Know

While the SOM is known the world over as one of the greatest messages of all time, there are some today who debate how it should be understood and applied.

Was it merely a transcript of a historical event? Was it a set of aspirational (albeit unrealistic) goals for a perfect world far off in the future? Or could it be convicting and applicable to everyone everywhere in every time and every place?

(Spoiler alert: it's that last one.)

In Matthew's summary, the SOM closes with a twice-repeated invitation for "everyone then who hears these words of mine" (Matt. 7:24, 26)—which strongly implies Jesus's message was universal.

It's difficult to argue that Matthew took time to record this repeated exhortation (along with the rest of the SOM, for that matter) believing it only applied to the people who were present that day.

And so, we believe the SOM is not only for historical curiosity and future anticipation; the SOM was, in fact, intended to make a difference in how all of Jesus's followers—in all times and places—live their lives.

You've Heard It Said

"You have heard that it was said to those of old, 'You shall not murder;
and whoever murders will be liable to judgment.' But I say to you that
everyone who is angry with his brother will be liable to judgment;
whoever insults his brother will be liable to the council; and whoever
says, 'You fool!' will be liable to the hell of fire. So if you are offering
your gift at the altar and there remember that your brother has
something against you, leave your gift there before the altar and go.
First be reconciled to your brother, and then come and offer your gift."

Matthew 5:21–24

Whenever Jesus started a sentence with "you've heard it said," His listeners were about to have their worlds rocked. Because it's pretty easy to avoid being a murderer—most people read the sixth commandment and put a checkmark in the corresponding box.

But as it turns out, the absence of murder doesn't mean our hearts are free from the darkness that births it. Which means Jesus's take on the sixth commandment makes it much harder to keep since it's nearly impossible to go through life without ever holding a grudge. Or having one held against you.

Commandment VI:
You shall not murder.

Grudge:
a persistent feeling of ill will or resentment resulting from a past insult or injury.

For Bible Nerds (like us) Who Want to Know

What scholars call the "antitheses" section of the SOM (Matt. 5:21–48) contains six repetitions of the theme "You have heard it said …, but I say to you …" (vv. 21–22, 27–28, 31–32, 33–34, 38–39, 43–44).

These are places where Jesus corrected misunderstandings about the Old Testament. Mind you, He was not correcting the Old Testament, which He made clear by saying, "Do not think that I have come to abolish the Law or the Prophets; I have not come to abolish them but to fulfill them" (v. 17).

Rather, Jesus was correcting the people's interpretations of God's Word and the way they put it into practice.

Perhaps that's why Jesus spoke of forgiveness so often. In the week before He was crucified, He said, "Whenever you stand praying, forgive, if you have anything against anyone, so that your Father also who is in heaven may forgive you your trespasses" (Mark 11:25). And then He proceeded to forgive the very people who nailed Him to the cross. "Father, forgive them, for they know not what they do" (Luke 23:34).

How is that possible?

Well, in our measly sinful strength, it's not. And yet the Bible tells us that in order to have fellowship with God, our accounts must be clear. In order to receive forgiveness from God, we must extend radical grace to others. In order to experience the peace of God, we must trust Him to avenge. And in order to interact with others the way God wants us to, we must wholly depend on the sinless, steadfast, and unconditional love of the One we follow.

Your Turn

2. Are you holding or have you ever held a grudge? Against who and why?

"God is light, and in him is no darkness at all. If we say we have fellowship with him while we walk in darkness, we lie and do not practice the truth … [But] if we confess our sins, he is faithful and just to forgive us our sins and to cleanse us from all unrighteousness."
1 John 1:5–6, 9

"Judge not, and you will not be judged; condemn not, and you will not be condemned; forgive, and you will be forgiven … For with the measure you use it will be measured back to you."
Luke 6:37–38

"If possible, so far as it depends on you, live peaceably with all. Beloved, never avenge yourselves, but leave it to the wrath of God, for it is written, 'Vengeance is mine, I will repay, says the Lord.' To the contrary, 'if your enemy is hungry, feed him; if he is thirsty, give him something to drink; for by so doing you will heap burning coals on his head.'"
Romans 12:18–20

Avenge:
to accomplish justice by punishing wrongdoing.

3. Read Matthew 18:21–35. While you can't earn God's forgiveness through good behavior, why does God's forgiveness depend on your willingness to forgive others?

4. Based on the parable Jesus told in Luke 7:41–50, explain the following statement:

Those who are forgiven much, love much. Those who are forgiven little, love little.

East and West

"He does not deal with us according to our sins, nor repay us according to our iniquities. For as high as the heavens are above the earth, so great is his steadfast love toward those who fear him; as far as the east is from the west, so far does he remove our transgressions from us. As a father shows compassion to his children, so the LORD shows compassion to those who fear him. For he knows our frame; he remembers that we are dust."

Psalm 103:10–14

Entitled: believing oneself to be inherently deserving of privileges or special treatment.

We tend to be an entitled people. Meaning, most of us think we deserve more respect and greater consideration than we sometimes get. At the same time, we minimize our flaws, believing them to be fewer and farther between *and more justifiable* than the flaws of those around us. And under the right conditions, those thoughts can morph into the grudges we hold against people we believe have done us wrong.

Yet the Bible repeatedly tells us that God doesn't deal with us that way. Instead, He offers to forgive our trespasses and remove our sin from us, as far as the east is from the west. Comprehending the magnitude of such grace, such grandiose mercy and love, requires a greater understanding of (a) our own sin, (b) what we actually deserve, and (c) what God did for us instead.

Contrary to our sense of entitlement, we're very sinful people. Our hearts are prone to wander away from God—to choose the wide road. To be self-centered, self-promoting, and self-indulgent. To be lustful and greedy for gain. To be disrespectful, discontent, and disconnected from the truth. To be angry, judgmental, and yes, unforgiving.

And God sees it all but pursues us anyway. "For he knows our frame; he remembers that we are dust." In spite of our sin and the righteous judgment it deserves, God withholds that judgment from those who follow Jesus because Jesus took it instead! Thus, God is both righteous and compassionate. He knows we're weak and frail. He knows our lives on earth are fleeting.

Like dust.

Indeed, during the course of our lives, each one of us will experience struggle and sickness, heartbreak, pain, and ultimately death—along with our ongoing inability to NOT sin. But none of these calamities go unseen by the One who loved us enough to take the consequence of our sin upon Himself. The Bible says:

The Romans Road (not an actual road; rather, it's a series of verses from the New Testament book of Romans that lays out God's plan of salvation):

"For all have sinned and fall short of the glory of God." Romans 3:23

"But God shows his love for us in that while we were still sinners, Christ died for us." Romans 5:8

"For the wages of sin is death, but the free gift of God is eternal life in Christ Jesus our Lord." Romans 6:23

"If you confess with your mouth that Jesus is Lord and believe in your heart that God raised him from the dead, you will be saved. For with the heart one believes and is justified, and with the mouth one confesses and is saved." Romans 10:9–10

For Bible Nerds (like us) Who Want to Know

As followers of Jesus, we're instructed to be forgiving. "Put on then, as God's chosen ones, holy and beloved, compassionate hearts, kindness, humility, meekness, and patience, bearing with one another and, if one has a complaint against another, forgiving each other; as the Lord has forgiven you, so you also must forgive" (Col. 3:12–13).

Of course, God doesn't force His forgiveness upon us: that is, a person can choose to not believe in Jesus and to not receive God's forgiveness in Christ. In which case, God doesn't hold a grudge. Rather, He allows people to continue down the path of destruction. And so, even as God—with great sorrow—lets unrepentant unbelievers go their own way, sometimes we too will have to let people go.

On that note, while it's true we're called to be like Jesus and to offer forgiveness to others, that doesn't mean we have to live under continued abuse by those who are unrepentant.

If you find yourself in a troublesome or dangerous situation where you can't discern what offering forgiveness looks like, by all means, seek the wisdom of a trusted pastor or other Christian leader.

He made you (Ps. 139:13).

He knows the number of hairs on your head (Matt. 10:30).

He knows when you sit and when you rise, and discerns your thoughts (Ps. 139:2).

He counts your tears and keeps track of your sorrows (Ps. 56:8).

He heals the brokenhearted and binds up wounds (Ps. 147:3).

Such knowledge should melt our self-focused, self-protective, hard hearts. Our sin offends the Lord, but He forgives and heals and draws near to those who draw near to Him (James 4:8). So, what right do we have to hold others to a standard we're not being held to? On the contrary, when we truly grasp the height and width and length and breadth of God's goodness toward us, we can't help but forgive those who've trespassed against us.

At least, in theory.

Your Turn

5. Some have defined compassion as sympathetic pity or sadness for the suffering of others, accompanied by a desire to relieve it. How does the Romans Road (see page 25) outline God's compassion?

6. God knows your comings and goings, intimately understands your sorrow, and forgives you every time you ask. How does that make you feel?

7. Psalm 139 closes with these words: "Search me, O God, and know my heart! Try me and know my thoughts! And see if there be any grievous way in me, and lead me in the way everlasting!" (vv. 23–24). Pray those words and confess anything God brings to mind.

Shalom

"You have heard that it was said, 'An eye for an eye and a tooth
for a tooth.' But I say to you, Do not resist the one who is evil.
But if anyone slaps you on the right cheek, turn to him the other
also. And if anyone would sue you and take your tunic, let him
have your cloak as well. And if anyone forces you to go one mile,
go with him two miles. Give to the one who begs from you,
and do not refuse the one who would borrow from you."
Matthew 5:38–42

Some things are harder to forgive than others. Obviously. That said, nothing is more difficult to forgive than murder. And Jesus was murdered. But instead of calling down the wrath of heaven—which He had every right and the ability to do (understatement)—Jesus asked God to forgive the people who were mocking, torturing, and killing Him (Luke 23:34).

He turned His cheek. And He's who we follow.

We're called to forgive as our Lord and Savior forgives (Col. 3:12–13), trusting that when we do, He'll be the One to avenge, protect, comfort, and heal us. This makes our forgiveness of others an act of faith that God sees and cares for us, that He uses all things for our good and His glory (Rom. 8:28).

Of course, in our measly, sinful strength, it is indeed an impossible exhortation. But Jesus said, "What is impossible with man is possible with God" (Luke 18:27)! By way of the narrow gate, He has offered us His *shalom*: peace with Him and peace with others. Oh, that we'd trust Him enough to walk through the gate, to let Him fully care for us, and to allow Him so much access to our hearts that He'd complete the work of forgiveness in and through us.

> Shalom:
> a Hebrew salutation used by Jewish people at meeting or parting, meaning peace, wholeness, completeness, soundness, health, safety, and prosperity, carrying with it the implication of permanence.

Your Turn

8. No one is a mature follower of Jesus when they first come to faith. Read Philippians 1:6. Over time, and as we follow Jesus, what does the Bible promise God will do?

Prayer Focus

Praise God for loving you as His creation despite your sinfulness, for sending Jesus to be the sacrifice for that sin, and for extending radical grace and forgiveness to you. Ask Him to help you do the hard work of forgiving others. Remember, forgiveness is sometimes a process—we don't always get there right away, which means we have to keep bringing our struggle and pain to the Lord each day. Thank Him for His promise to change your heart when you do, and for His faithfulness to make you more and more like Jesus.

Sample Prayer

Dear God,

Thank You for loving me even though I have been rebellious against You—sometimes in my heart and sometimes in my actions. Thank You for sending Jesus to provide the way of salvation, and to restore me to a right relationship with You. I acknowledge I can't earn Your forgiveness and must receive it as a gift paid for by Jesus. Thank You that Your forgiveness can change my life, including the way I respond to others. Give me the ability to forgive and the courage to ask for forgiveness when I'm the one who needs it. "Restore to me the joy of your salvation, and uphold me with a willing spirit," so I can invite others to do the same (Ps. 51:12).

Amen.

EXT. MARY MAGDALENE'S APARTMENT (DAY)

(Andrew approaches the front door and knocks. After a moment, Mary opens.)

MARY MAGDALENE *(confused)*: Shalom.

ANDREW: Shalom. I won't take much time.

MARY MAGDALENE: It's fine. Do you need anything?

ANDREW: I just want to say something. In Rabbi's sermon, He said to reconcile with someone first before worshipping. And I need to apologize to you.

MARY MAGDALENE: You don't owe me—

ANDREW: Yes, I do. I said awful things to you because I was scared, which Rabbi also talked about. He talked about many things. I've got a lot to work on, actually.

MARY MAGDALENE: Me too.

ANDREW: But I said awful things to you. You didn't deserve it. And I'm really sorry. *(Mary smiles.)*

ANDREW (CONT'D): So … that's all.

MARY MAGDALENE: I'm sorry, I'm not sure what to say. I think this is the first time anyone's ever said sorry to me for anything.

ANDREW: You don't deserve that, either … Things are better now, huh?

MARY MAGDALENE: Yes. A lot. Thank you for this.

ANDREW: Shalom.

MARY MAGDALENE: Shalom.

"And Jesus came and said to them, 'All authority in heaven and on earth has been given to me. Go therefore and make disciples of all nations, baptizing them in the name of the Father and of the Son and of the Holy Spirit, teaching them to observe all that I have commanded you. And behold, I am with you always, to the end of the age.'"

Matthew 28:18–20

Lesson 2

GO
as Jesus sends you

INT. SIMON'S HOUSE (NIGHT)

(Simon and Eden hold each other, watching a fire. They're all alone, not talking. Finally, after a while ...)

EDEN: I can't believe I have you back.

SIMON: I don't believe you don't believe. Here I am. Where I'll always be.

EDEN: When you were gone this time, I had moments of feeling ...

SIMON: Feeling what?

EDEN: Lost ... I don't know what to call them.

SIMON: What did they feel like?

EDEN: I was angry. Sad ...

SIMON: Oh, love. You know I'm with Jesus. We both are. Do you remember what He told you?

EDEN: I always remember that. It's what gets me through the days.

SIMON: He sees you.

EDEN: I know. I think of that moment so often. But sometimes, in the memory, I forget what His face looks like.

SIMON: What do you mean?

EDEN: Haven't you ever been separated from someone and you can't recall their face after a while?

SIMON: Do you forget my face? *(Eden laughs at his selfish, childish wonderfulness.)*

EDEN: I don't forget your face. *(sinking into him)* Things are so good now.

SIMON: We just have to spend more time together. You know? I think Jesus has work to do here. *(after a beat)* I've been thinking about … our family.

EDEN *(shrugs)*: *Eema* is healthy, my brothers are fishing—

SIMON: No, *our* family. *(Eden turns to look at him. Wide eyed—)*

SIMON (CONT'D): It's time. *(She throws her arms around Simon, overcome.)*

"Joshua fought the battle of Jericho, and the walls came tumblin' down."

♫

"Zacchaeus was a wee little man, and a wee little man was he."

♪

"The Lord told Noah there's gonna be a floody floody, get those animals out of the muddy muddy, children of the Lord."

♫

"Children, go where I send thee,
How shall I send thee?
I'm gonna send thee eight by eight,
Eight for the eight that
stood at the gate,
Seven for the seven came
down from heaven,
Six for the six that couldn't get fixed,
Five for the gospel preacher,
Four for the poor that
stood at the door,
Three for the Hebrew children,
Two for Paul and Silas,
One for the little biddy baby—
He was born, born, born
in Bethlehem."

Plans

Sometimes we forget the disciples were real people. We read Scripture in a way that causes all their humanity to drain from the page. We say Bible verses by rote and sing Sunday school songs that don't quite capture the real stories. Even our paintings and beautiful stained-glass windows can make Jesus and His followers seem flat and distant and disconnected from our twenty-first-century reality.

As in, "That was then. This is now."

And so, sometimes we think they had less to lose. Quite literally. After all, the men and women who dropped everything to follow Jesus had less stuff than most of us do now. They didn't have cars or mortgages or college loans to pay off. They certainly didn't have as many options for where to live, work, or go on vacation. Incidentally, they also didn't have smartphones, social media, and twenty-four-hour news cycles giving them up-to-the-minute information on absolutely everything and everyone.

Their lives were simpler. Or so we tell ourselves.

But that didn't make their plans any easier to abandon.

On the contrary. Because as it turns out, there's
nothing new under the sun—not when it comes to the
human experience. While the disciples' circumstances were
different from ours, people are still people, regardless of the
time they're born into history.

> "What has been will be again,
> what has been done
> will be done again;
> there is nothing new
> under the sun."
> Ecclesiastes 1:9 (NIV)

Which means the followers of Jesus had families and whole communities they loved.
They had ambition, hope, and plans for the future. They experienced happiness and stress,
love and heartbreak, excitement and confusion, courage and fear.

In all those ways, they were just like us.

So, of course, when Jesus said "go," it took 'em a minute.

Your Turn

1. What plans for your life do you hold most dear?

Two by Two

"And he called the twelve and began to send them out two by two,
and gave them authority over the unclean spirits. He charged them
to take nothing for their journey except a staff—no bread, no bag, no
money in their belts—but to wear sandals and not put on two tunics."

Mark 6:7–9

For Bible Nerds (like us) Who Want to Know

Not all of the disciples were apostles. Disciples of Jesus are people who are devoted to following Him, which means Jesus had crowds of disciples during His earthly ministry, and millions of them since! The apostles were twelve of Jesus's disciples whom He selected to be leaders among the rest.

At the time of this particular missions trip, many disciples had been with Jesus for some time, and at the Sermon on the Mount, He gave twelve of them the role and title of "apostle." This label comes from the Greek word meaning "one who is sent."

How cool is that?

The Gospel of Luke records Jesus sending His followers out two by two on a second short-term missions trip, only this one was for a bigger group of seventy-two disciples (Luke 10:1–12). The difference between the first and second trips was …

Those were pretty specific and also terrifying marching orders. The apostles were being sent into the countryside to do what, until that point, they'd only been watching Jesus do. But now they were supposed to do it themselves without food or shelter. Or innate power. Jesus was asking them to trust His word that provision for all the above would manifest as needed.

Of course, unlike road trips today, there weren't pit stops along the way. There weren't exits every few miles with options for snacks, bathrooms, and hotels. Goodness, even with the ability to stop and refuel at will, we *still* pack snacks. But these guys were told to set out with nothing but the shirts on their backs and the sandals on their feet. They couldn't even bring an extra staff, which would've been used as both a walking stick through tough terrain and a self-defense weapon against wild animals and bad guys (Matt. 10:9–10).

Boiled down, the plan was "take nothing because you'll be provided for in your hour of need." But in spite of the unknown and all the scary scenarios that came with it, they went as they were told. Just imagine the first day of that journey—the amount of faith they must've had in Jesus to take the initial steps. No supplies, no plan other than walking and preaching and healing, which none of them had ever done before.

It's remarkable they didn't all defect then and there.

Your Turn

2. When it comes to your plans, are you hoping God blesses what *you* want to do? Or has what you want to do been authored by God? Incidentally, how can you tell the difference?

3. Read Jeremiah 29:11; Psalm 32:8; and Romans 8:28. What do these verses indicate about God's plans for you?

4. When the apostles were sent two by two, the entirety of the plan was to trust God's provision. What do you suppose the men were feeling? Why do you suppose they went anyway?

The Kingdom Is at Hand

"Jesus came into Galilee, proclaiming the gospel of God,
and saying, 'The time is fulfilled, and the kingdom
of God is at hand; repent and believe in the gospel.'"

Mark 1:14–15

As scary as it was for the twelve apostles to embrace the unknown, their stepping out in faith was also understandable because they were experiencing the kingdom of God! After all, they'd seen Jesus restore the sick, lame, and possessed. They witnessed Him calm storms and raise the dead. They felt the words He spoke breathe life and light into their very souls, and they would never be the same.

Indeed, when Jesus said "the time is fulfilled," He was talking about Himself: the promised Messiah the people of God had been waiting for, the fulfillment of Old Testament prophecy, the One who would restore the ruins and replant the wastelands, the Savior who would take upon Himself all that had been destroyed in Eden.

Heaven had come to earth and Jesus's followers knew it. How could they refuse to go when and where *and how* He sent them?

How could we?

As it turns out, the combination of take nothing / receive everything is a winning one—the disciples saw people healed, body and soul. And just like them, when we offer ourselves to Jesus, He faithfully works in and through us to accomplish what we could never accomplish in our own power or wildest dreams.

But it starts with being sent.

Your Turn

5. When it comes to our plans, we often wonder what we'll miss if we go God's way instead of our own. Now turn that idea upside down and make a list of what the disciples would've missed had they *not* gone when and how Jesus sent them.

6. Romans 12:1–2 tells us to present ourselves as a living sacrifice in order to be transformed by Jesus and thus better able to discern God's will. What might *you* miss if you refuse Him?

7. Read Mark 1:14–15 and Matthew 10:5–7. What does the "kingdom of God" (or the "kingdom of heaven") refer to? What is the connection between God being a king and His people being repentant?

Kingdom Caveat

"And he said to them, 'Whenever you enter a house, stay there until you depart from there. And if any place will not receive you and they will not listen to you, when you leave, shake off the dust that is on your feet as a testimony against them.'"

Mark 6:10–11

Jesus promised His apostles provision for the journey and power for the work He was sending them to do, but that didn't

---

For Bible Nerds (like us) Who Want to Know

The idea of God being king over all creation and especially over His people has roots in the Old Testament (Deut. 33:5; Ps. 99:1–5; Isa. 6:1–5).

But in addition to statements about God's present kingship, there are implications for a more robust future kingdom of God (Isa. 24:21–23; 33:17–22; Zech. 14:1–9). Jesus announced that this future kingdom was breaking into reality ("the kingdom of God is at hand") through His life and work.

Of course, God's reign has already begun in the hearts and lives of those with faith in Jesus (Luke 11:20; 17:20–21; 18:16–17), even though it's not yet fully consummated and won't be until Jesus comes again (Luke 13:28–30; 19:11; 21:31; 22:16–18).

And so, in our present day and age, scholars refer to this idea as the "already/not yet" kingdom of God.

mean smooth sailing. On the contrary, He warned His followers that they would be well-received by some and rejected by others.

Just like He was.

Just like He is still.

In fact, part of His provision is actually to manage our expectations. Because as we represent Jesus and His mind-blowing, heart-changing, life-upending kingdom, we should expect to experience the same kinds of things He and the early disciples did. When the kingdom of heaven is well-received, we should rejoice and praise God. But when it's rejected, we shouldn't be surprised or shaken because, either way, we still belong to the kingdom.

Indeed, we're sent by the King. At the end of His time on earth, Jesus commissioned His followers (which includes us!) to go into the world with the true message of salvation. In fact, Matthew closes his gospel account with what has come to be known as the Great Commission: "All authority in heaven and on earth has been given to me. Go therefore and make disciples of all nations, baptizing them in the name of the Father and of the Son and of the Holy Spirit, teaching them to observe all that I have commanded you. And behold, I am with you always, to the end of the age" (Matt. 28:18–20).

The Great Commission: the instruction of the resurrected Jesus Christ to His disciples to spread the gospel to all the nations of the world.

So, yeah, it's pretty great.

Your Turn

8. What new thing are you sensing God wants to do in and through you today? Are there any people or places you think God may be sending you to with the gospel message? What concerns do you have about how the particulars of the assignment get accomplished?

Prayer Focus

Praise God for including you in His kingdom plans. Thank Him for promising to provide the food, money, power, and words you're going to need to do the work. Ask Him to grow your faith so that when, where, and how He sends you, you'll willingly go.

Sample Prayer

Dear God,

Thank You for sending Jesus to announce Your kingdom that has come to earth through His life and work. Thank You for bringing me into Your kingdom through repentance and faith in Jesus. You have chosen to continue Your kingdom work through followers of Jesus like me. But I'm not always sure about when, where, or how to best carry out Your work. Please guide me and help me respond well to Your guidance (Ps. 32:8–11). You have promised to provide for me, so help me put Your kingdom first (Matt. 6:25–34). Please give me compassion for those who will hear me, courage to speak the gospel message boldly, and wise words.

Amen.

INT. SIMON'S HOUSE (DAY)

(The disciples and Jesus are crammed into the too-small living room of Simon and Eden's home. Eden comes in and out with food.)

JESUS: I'm sure by now most of you are aware of the tent village that is rapidly growing west of Capernaum. *(Sounds of affirmation emerge from the group.)* Those are people who followed us from the Mount, and who are now waiting to hear more. Their numbers grow by the day, as does the suspicions of Rome. Zee has informed Me just this morning that some members of his former order have even journeyed here.

ANDREW: It would appear as if we were building an army, Teacher.

JESUS: I suppose that's one way to look at it. *(Everyone glances all around. Intrigued, worried, confused.)*

JESUS (CONT'D): The other way to look at it is My way.

SIMON: The correct way, You mean.

JESUS *(chuckling)*: Yes, Simon. Those people are like those in regions all over. They are not an army. Not now. They are in need of rescue. And you are going to help Me rescue them. *(Zee pounds his fist and leans forward. Simon nods at him.)*

JESUS (CONT'D): Different kind of rescue, Zee. It is not sustainable for Me to do all the preaching, all the healing, and the ministering. I called you to Simon's home today, and thank you, Eden, for hosting us, because our ministry will only grow, and we want it to grow till the end of the age. There will be many more followers, and like those not here, they will all have roles and responsibilities. Most will be disciples, students. But I have chosen you twelve as my apostles. *(The disciples are quiet. This is big. After a moment …)*

BIG JAMES: You're sending us?

MATTHEW: An apostle is the same as a messenger, one who—

BIG JAMES: I know what it means, Matthew, that's why I'm asking.

JESUS: You are My leaders. And for the mission I have for you, it's best that you spread out and not be concentrated in one place.

ANDREW: I don't understand.

JESUS: I'm going to go home to Nazareth for a time, and while I'm there, I am sending you out, in every direction, two by two. *(The room is silent. Every single person is convinced they misheard.)*

THOMAS *(Filled with dread. He had plans.)*: Every direction, Rabbi?

JESUS: You will proclaim, as you go—"The kingdom of heaven is at hand." And while you are on this mission, you will heal the sick and lame by anointing them with oil, you will cast out demons … Why are you all looking at Me like that?

MATTHEW: Could You just repeat that one more time?

JESUS: I am sending you out, two by two, proclaiming as you go—"The kingdom of heaven is at hand." Heal the sick, cast out demons …

SIMON *(exchanging a look with Eden)*: How soon are we talking about here?

JESUS: There's that word again. We will get to that, Simon.

PHILIP: Heal the sick?

(We get a glimpse of Little James.)

THADDAEUS: Cast out demons?

JESUS: While you're on this mission, you will have this authority. Someday you will have it all the time.

NATHANAEL: Was there a ceremony I missed?

JESUS: This is it.

NATHANAEL: I don't feel any different.

JESUS: I don't need you to feel anything to do great things.

JOHN: With all due respect, Rabbi, we've only just begun as students, we're not nearly qualified, why would You need us for this work?

ZEE: He doesn't need us, He wants us.

JESUS: Very good, Zee. John, if I needed religious leaders and qualified students for My ministry, I wouldn't have chosen—well, you get the point.

"The Spirit of the Lord is upon me, because he has anointed me to proclaim good news to the poor. He has sent me to proclaim liberty to the captives and recovering of sight to the blind, to set at liberty those who are oppressed, to proclaim the year of the Lord's favor."

Luke 4:18–19

GRIEVE
as Jesus grieves

EXT. NAZARETH STREET (DUSK) SUPER: Nazareth, AD 27

(Jesus turns onto a Nazareth street, strolls a few moments, and then stops in front of a small house. After a pause, He smiles, and then approaches the door and knocks. Immediately—)

MOTHER MARY: Oh! I'm coming! If it's You, come in, but I'm coming! *(Jesus chuckles but waits. After a beat, the door opens.)*

MOTHER MARY (CONT'D): Oh yes, it's You! *L'shana tovah!*

JESUS: *L'shana tovah*, Eema.

MOTHER MARY *(hugging Him)*: Why didn't You just come in, You know You can just come in? Did You have a good journey, You look tired. You're hungry, yes? We'll sit and eat. You can just set Your bag down there, we'll eat first and then You can go to bed, I'm sure You're exhausted. The challah is hot and ready, Your timing is perfect. Did You have a good journey?

JESUS: Yes, it was fine. I saw the brown dog wasn't at the city gate when I got in, did something happen?

MOTHER MARY: He died several months ago. Sit, sit …

JESUS: Ah, I figured. I don't think I've walked through that gate in ten years without seeing him sitting nearby being ignored by everyone.

L'shana tovah:
the Hebrew phrase
for "good year."

(Mother pulls the round challah out of the oven and brings it to the place setting, then sits while whispering a prayer.)

MOTHER MARY: It's not perfectly round, I've never been able to do it perfect, but the raisins cooked in nicely.

JESUS: Eema, you know I don't like raisins.

MOTHER MARY: And You know I'm going to do it for a sweet new year anyway, so hush.

JESUS: So … no Jude and James?

MOTHER MARY *(pursing her lips … this is clearly an uncomfortable topic)*: Well … they felt it best to celebrate in Haifa while You were here. Just to avoid conflict.

JESUS: I understand.

MOTHER MARY: I think it's just hard for them, especially with so many people here excited to see You tomorrow. Everyone has been hearing about what You've been doing, the signs and wonders, and You know how the boys feel about all that.

JESUS: I understand.

MOTHER MARY *(covering)*: But we'll have a lovely time. How is the bread?

JESUS: It's wonderful, and I even like the raisins.

MOTHER MARY: So … are You ready for tomorrow? So many have told me they can't wait to see You. And guess who is in town?

JESUS: I couldn't tell you.

MOTHER MARY: Lazarus and the sisters. They got in today, they figured it was a good opportunity to see You.

JESUS: Really? That's wonderful, I haven't seen Laz in a while. So … I'm exhausted, I need to get to bed. Eema …

MOTHER MARY: Yes?

JESUS: I need the box while I'm here. Where do you have it?

MOTHER MARY *(her countenance changes)*: Now?

JESUS: Mmhm.

MOTHER MARY: You're sure this is Your last time here before …

JESUS: I believe My time is coming.

MOTHER MARY (*deeply saddened*): I don't know that I'm ready.

JESUS: I know how you feel. But I do the—

MOTHER MARY: —will of Him who sent Me. JESUS: —will of Him who sent Me.

MOTHER MARY: Does it have to be so soon? Are You sure?

JESUS: If not now …

MOTHER MARY (*quietly*): I miss Your father the most during celebrations. He had so much fun. It'll be a fun day tomorrow. The box is near Your bed. You'll see it.

JESUS: Thank you.

MOTHER MARY: I'll clean up, You go to bed.

JESUS: I can help you …

MOTHER MARY (*trying to avoid emotion*): No, I've got it, go to bed, I'll be fine. (*As she turns toward the kitchen area, Jesus puts His arm around her and kisses her on the head.*)

JESUS: *Laila tov*, Eema.

Laila tov:
the Hebrew phrase for
"good night."

The Reason He Came

In a quiet synagogue in His small hometown of Nazareth, Jesus made an announcement so enormous and shocking, the hearers (i.e., His lifelong friends and neighbors) tried throwing Him off a cliff. Apparently, in first-century Israel that was what you did when someone claimed to be the long-awaited Messiah, Savior of the Jews, and the One through whom God's favor would be poured out on the whole wide world:

Messiah:
the promised deliverer of the
Jewish nation prophesied
in the Old Testament.

And [Jesus] rolled up the scroll and gave it back to the attendant and sat down. And the eyes of all in the synagogue were fixed on him. And he began to say to them, "Today this Scripture has been fulfilled in your hearing." (Luke 4:20–21)

But let's back up lest we miss the forest for the murderous trees. Because when Jesus read the Old Testament scroll of Isaiah, He was revealing God's heart for the people He made. He was expressing His deep love and compassion for a hurting world. He was unveiling God's plan to restore what had been lost, chained, broken, and buried by sin.

Indeed, Jesus came to bring good news to the poor, liberty to captives, sight to the blind, and freedom to the oppressed. He came to turn mourning into joy and helplessness into hopefulness that would stretch into eternity. He came to bind up earthly wounds and heal broken hearts. He came to rescue and restore a grief-stricken, heavy-laden, and weary world.

Gentile:
a person who is not Jewish.

Including the Gentiles.

And including you.

Your Turn

1. Read Matthew 9:35–36; Mark 3:1–5; and John 11:17, 34–36. What are some things that grieve Jesus's heart?

All the Things

"When they heard these things, all in the synagogue were
filled with wrath. And they rose up and drove him out of
the town and brought him to the brow of the hill on which
their town was built, so that they could throw him down the
cliff. But passing through their midst, he went away."

Luke 4:28–30

In episode 3, season 3 of *The Chosen*, Jesus goes home for a visit and Mother Mary is excited. But joy quickly turns to sorrow when Jesus asks about His brothers, and Mary has to explain that they aren't coming because they don't approve of Jesus. Of course, those specific details are creatively licensed for the show, but we do know from Scripture that Joseph and Mary had other children (Matt. 13:55–56; Mark 6:3) and "not even his brothers believed in him" (John 7:5)—at least, not during Jesus's earthly ministry. Furthermore, it seems Joseph had already died, since he's not mentioned at any point during Jesus's ministry. In fact, while on the cross, Jesus assigned John the task of caring for Mary (John 19:26–27).

And all of that means things like death, division, rejection, and even estrangement are griefs Jesus intimately understands.

The episode moves on to depict the actual sermon Jesus preaches in His hometown of Nazareth, where trouble extends beyond His family (Luke 4:16–30). To the horror of His hometown, Jesus insists on God's love for all people and His plan to include and redeem the Gentiles. Tragically, cultural prejudice is so deeply ingrained in their way of life, they become enraged and accuse Jesus of being a false prophet and speaking blasphemy.

False prophet:
a person who spreads false teachings while claiming to speak the Word of God.

Blasphemy:
the act or offense of speaking sacrilegiously about God or sacred things; profane talk.

Sacrilege:
violation or misuse of what is regarded as sacred.

For Bible Nerds (like us) Who Want to Know

The people of Nazareth were upset when Jesus claimed to be the Messiah. But they became even more enraged when He implied that God's plan of salvation included the Gentiles (Luke 4:24–27).

In OT Israelite law, that language was viewed as blasphemous false prophecy, and blasphemy was punishable by death (Lev. 24:10–16; compare with Deut. 13:6–11). The Jewish rabbinic document known as the Mishnah actually describes a proper stoning procedure, which included throwing a person over a cliff and dropping stones on him or her.

That said, such a punishment was only supposed to be carried out after a proper trial (Deut. 17:2–7), not through mob violence as seen in Luke 4:28–29 (and as threatened in John 8:59 and 10:31–33). Moreover, under Roman rule, capital punishment was *only* supposed to be carried out with the government's permission (John 18:31)—though there were times when the Jews bent that rule (for example, with Stephen in Acts 7:54–58 and the attempt on Paul's life in Acts 21:31–32).

Besides skipping a proper Jewish trial and moving ahead without Roman permission, it was odd for the Jews of Nazareth to rush into doing the "work" of stoning Jesus on the Sabbath, especially since breaking the Sabbath was, ironically, also punishable by death (Num. 15:32–36).

Fast-forward to the cliff, and imagine the scene from God's perspective. To see Scripture misunderstood and misused on such a grand scale; to see rebellion and outright disobedience to His will and way; to witness such callous disregard for His unfailing love, patience, and mercy; to watch an angry mob drag His beloved Son up a hill.

It wouldn't be the last time.

Oh, how that day must've hurt the heart of the One who was watching—the One who sees everything, all the time. Because as it turns out, nothing escapes God's purview; no evil thing remains a secret. On the contrary, every twisted, terrible thing we humans do to ourselves and to each other is ever before Him.

And He grieves.

Your Turn

2. Here's the answer to question 1: Jesus grieves when people are lost. He grieves when people hurt each other. He grieves when people grieve. In other words, what is the source of His grief?

3. Read John 3:16–17. What did God's love and grief lead Him to do?

4. Consider the world and its current condition from God's point of view.

That's all.

Just take a crushing moment to consider it.

Man of Sorrows

"For he grew up before him like a young plant, and like a root out of dry ground; he had no form or majesty that we should look at him, and no beauty that we should desire him. He was despised and rejected by men, a man of sorrows and acquainted with grief; and as one from whom men hide their faces he was despised, and we esteemed him not. Surely he has borne our griefs and carried our sorrows; yet we esteemed him stricken, smitten by God, and afflicted."

Isaiah 53:2–4

Jesus entered into His creation, subjecting Himself to all the brokenness and pain that came with it in order to save us from it. He was plain and poor, overlooked and unesteemed. He was despised. Rejected. He, in fact, became our grief, taking our sorrow and God's righteous judgment for sin upon Himself. Which means there's no pain in life He doesn't intimately understand, no burden He hasn't felt the weight of. The Bible refers to Him as a man of sorrows, acquainted *in every way* with grief.

Including yours.

To that end, grief isn't something we should fear or deny or even always avoid. On the contrary, Jesus promises that in this world we're going to have trouble.

"God shows his love for us in that while we were still sinners, Christ died for us."
Romans 5:8

"Since then we have a great high priest who has passed through the heavens, Jesus, the Son of God, let us hold fast our confession. For we do not have a high priest who is unable to sympathize with our weaknesses, but one who in every respect has been tempted as we are, yet without sin. Let us then with confidence draw near to the throne of grace, that we may receive mercy and find grace to help in time of need."
Hebrews 4:14–16

"In the world you will have
tribulation. But take heart; I
have overcome the world."
John 16:33

"The LORD is near to the brokenhearted
and saves the crushed in spirit."
Psalm 34:18

"Blessed be the God and Father of our
Lord Jesus Christ, the Father of mercies
and God of all comfort, who comforts
us in all our affliction, so that we may
be able to comfort those who are in any
affliction, with the comfort with which
we ourselves are comforted by God."
2 Corinthians 1:3–4

"[God] will wipe away every tear from
their eyes, and death shall be no more,
neither shall there be mourning, nor
crying, nor pain anymore, for the
former things have passed away."
Revelation 21:4

But He moves toward us in our grief, rescuing and comforting us, and offering hope for a day when sadness and suffering will be no more.

To know Jesus is to know the Comforter in Chief.

Once we know Him, we should grieve *with* Him and respond to others the way He does. That is to say, sin should break our hearts because it destroys God's perfect and beautiful creation. Lost people should break our hearts because they don't know their Creator or the love, forgiveness, and restoration He holds outstretched. And people perpetuating grief upon others should break our hearts because cycles of sin keep us from the One who promises to rescue and restore.

Your Turn

5. Explain how expecting troubles in life might help you cope with them differently.

6. How have you experienced God moving toward you in grief? How has His presence comforted you?

7. Reread the verses in the margin of this section. How does Jesus respond to our sin and grief, even when the latter is caused by the former? How do *you* typically respond to others' sin and grief?

Outside Eden

> "But he was pierced for our transgressions;
>
> he was crushed for our iniquities; upon
>
> him was the chastisement that brought us
>
> peace, and with his wounds we are healed."
>
> Isaiah 53:5

While it's true that mankind's road to destruction was paved in Eden, it's also true that grace upon grace has been poured out every day since, and ultimately in the person of Jesus Christ (John 1:16–17; Rom. 5:12–21). Which means God doesn't leave us stuck in our sin and grief. On the contrary, He made a way for us to be restored. Through the narrow gate, we find freedom. And while we'll never be entirely loose of pain or suffering on earth, when we walk with Jesus— the *Man of Sorrows*—we have all the empathy, care, and comfort that come with Him.

From our first step to our final breath.

For Bible Nerds (like us) Who Want to Know

Genesis 6:5–6 says, "The LORD saw that the wickedness of man was great in the earth, and that every intention of the thoughts of his heart was only evil continually. And the LORD regretted that he had made man on the earth, and it grieved him to his heart."

The idea that an omniscient (all-knowing) God could "regret" His own actions might be troubling for some readers. But this bold way of speaking anthropomorphically about God (ascribing human characteristics to a nonhuman) might help us understand how evil and upsetting sin really is.

Clearly, the "grief" God experiences is in response to the persistent, extensive, and intense sinfulness of humanity. The Hebrew word for "grieved" in Genesis 6:6 is in the same family of words as the "pain" Adam and Eve suffered as a result of sin in the Garden of Eden (Gen. 3:16–17).

While we certainly suffer the consequences of our sin, God is suffering too. His grief over human sin is expressed elsewhere in Scripture with the same grieving term (Ps. 78:40; Isa. 63:10). However, God has compassion on humans who suffer under the weight of sin, including and especially the sin we inflict on one another.

Using different terms than grief, God is described as having heard, seen, and known the afflictions of His people enslaved in Egypt (Ex. 2:23–25; 3:7–9). And so, He sent Moses to lead the Israelites out of Egypt, through the wilderness, and to the Promised Land.

Similarly, we see Messiah Jesus (the Savior and promised deliverer, prophesied of in the Old Testament) respond to the dire circumstances sinful people are in: "When he saw the crowds, he had compassion for them, because they were harassed and helpless, like sheep without a shepherd" (Matt. 9:36).

"Do not be anxious about anything, but in everything by prayer and supplication with thanksgiving let your requests be made known to God. And the peace of God, which surpasses all understanding, will guard your hearts and your minds in Christ Jesus" (Phil. 4:6–7).

When we surrender our confusion, pain, and grief to the Lord, His peace rushes in. His abundant mercy guards our hearts and overflows to the hurting people around us. His steadfast love compels us to keep putting one foot in front of the other, while His grace and goodness lead us out of bondage and toward the promised land of heaven (Ps. 23).

And there, God Himself will wipe away our tears.

Your Turn

8. Read Romans 8:18–39 and write down all the ways God's grace is greater than your grief.

Prayer Focus

Praise God for remaining present with you in grief. Thank Him for drawing near in spite of your sin and self-inflicted struggle, and for the narrow gate that leads to life. Ask for renewed strength and grace to keep moving forward and to follow Jesus no matter your circumstances. And pray for opportunities to extend God's grace and comfort to others.

Sample Prayer

Dear God,

I'm grieving today, but I'm also bringing it to You. Thank You that You've long been aware of my pain and that You choose to share in it. Thank You for sending Jesus to draw near to me, and to grieve with me, and that He made a way through and beyond my grief. I admit that some of my sadness comes from my own sinful choices. So, I thank You for Your forgiveness and Your promise to restore and make me new through Him. As I turn everything over to You, please help me bear up under them, trusting in You fully (Ps. 55:22; 1 Pet. 5:6–7; Matt. 6:25–34). Please change my heart to be grieved by what grieves You. And then grant me the love and grace to minister to others the way You want me to.

Amen.

INT. JOSEPH'S SHOP

(Joseph is in his place of business, building something as he talks to a six-year-old Jesus. Jesus is sitting on a little stool, reading from a scroll. It's clear He's learning.)

JESUS: "He has sent me to heal the … bro … keen … brokeen …"

JOSEPH: "Broken," then what?

JESUS: "Hee … hee are."

JOSEPH: Sound it out. All the letters.

JESUS: "Hee are teh … ted."

JOSEPH: Good, but now say it quickly.

JESUS: "Hee art ed."

JOSEPH: "Hearted." Now one word.

JESUS: "Brokenhearted." What does that mean?

JOSEPH: A heart that is broken. But not the heart in your chest. What makes you happy or sad. A broken heart means being sad or hurt, someone who needs help. Keep going.

JESUS: "To … pro … claim … proclaim … liberty."

JOSEPH: Good. Here, quick, hold this for me.

JESUS: I can help?

JOSEPH: Yes, come. *(Jesus hustles up next to Joseph, who hands Him a hammer.)* You need to learn how to do this well. In our family, we can strike a nail all the way through in one swing, *maybe* two. I'll allow You two on Your first try. *(He positions a nail in the right spot.)* Now, someday You won't be doing carpentry like me.

JESUS: Why, *Abba*?

JOSEPH: You'll be a craftsman, working with stone and other materials, not just wood.

JESUS: Why, Abba?

JOSEPH: Because there's not much wood around here, this is a place of rock and stone. I picked the wrong business, heh-heh. All right, here we go. Remember, You don't use Your whole big arm to swing. Just this part of Your arm, the bottom half. You just swing from Your elbow. This way You have more control, see? I will hold the nail steady so You don't hurt Yourself, and You swing. Ready?

JESUS: What if I hurt your hand?

JOSEPH: Oh, You have talent like Your Abba, You'll be fine. Go ahead.

(Jesus slowly does one or two practice motions, clearly concentrating hard and focused on the nail. He finally swings hard with His forearm and comes down on the nail. Joseph swipes his hand back.)

JOSEPH (CONT'D): OWWWW!!!!

(Jesus yells in shock and fear as Joseph rears back in "pain." But of course … Joseph bursts into laughter.)

JOSEPH (CONT'D): Just joking, ha-ha. That was great, look! The nail is halfway down. *(Joseph pulls Jesus close.)* I'm sorry, ha-ha, but I couldn't help it. Okay, I have something special I want to show You. Go get that box over there.

(Jesus gets it and Joseph opens it. It's the donkey bridle Jesus recovered from Mary's house.)

JOSEPH (CONT'D): Listen carefully, yes? This is a mule's bit and bridle. You've seen these before, but this is special. Thousands of years ago, when our people were finally set free from slavery … as they were leaving, one of our ancestors of the tribe of Judah used this very bit and bridle to lead his mule laden with supplies out of Egypt.

(Jesus notices Mother Mary has emerged in the doorframe, and she watches quietly, smiling.)

JOSEPH (CONT'D): Of course, the mule eventually died, and everything else was lost in the wilderness. But this bridle was in his hand when he escaped to freedom … so he kept it. The men in our family have handed it down to each other for more than forty generations as a remembrance of our bondage, but more importantly, in remembrance of being led to freedom into the Promised Land. It's old, and it's not beautiful, but my father handed it to me to own like I'm handing it to you. We always joked, "Who knows? Maybe one of us will need it one day." I don't suppose You will bear a son, so … maybe it will end its journey with You. But I can't leave this earth without passing it on.

JESUS *(staring at it, mesmerized)*: Thank you, Abba.

"Everyone then who hears these words of mine and does them will be like a wise man who built his house on the rock. And the rain fell, and the floods came, and the winds blew and beat on that house, but it did not fall, because it had been founded on the rock."

Matthew 7:24–25

Lesson 4

STAND
where Jesus stands

INT. SIMON'S HOME (DAY)

(All the disciples except Thomas gather at Simon's home. Each has returned from his mission. Like soldiers home from battle. Some haunted, others hardened. All changed.)

JOHN: And in an instant, just like that, her eyes went from gray to hazel. Thomas and I had never seen anything like it. The parents burst into tears.

ANDREW: It's a shame the first thing she had to see with her new eyes was you.

BIG JAMES: Traumatizing.

SIMON *(Absent from the banter, pouring water into jars. Next to him, Eden crushes soaked chickpeas.)*: Do you need any help with that?

EDEN *(coldly)*: No.

SIMON *(whispering)*: Has something been bothering you?

EDEN: No.

(Back to the boys.)

PHILIP: Turns out Andrew is truly a bold preacher.

ANDREW: I think we made a difference.

THADDAEUS: You were in the Decapolis with Gentiles?

PHILIP: Gentiles and Hellenistic Jews were around, yes. They hated us almost as much as they hate each other.

ANDREW: The Gentiles kicked us out, I think they thought we were helping start a war.

LITTLE JAMES: Simon, are you proud of your brother?

EDEN *(nudging him)*: Simon?

SIMON: I'm sorry, what?

LITTLE JAMES: I said you must be proud of your brother.

SIMON: Of course I am.

THADDAEUS: Big James, how was Ptolemais?

NATHANAEL: You've been quiet all morning.

LITTLE JAMES: Zee and Matthew, you too.

BIG JAMES *(shrugging)*: It was fine. We preached. We did what Jesus told us we now have the power to do.

NATHANAEL: You sound as enthusiastic as a Sadducee with a toothache.

BIG JAMES: I just don't know if it was a good idea. Just raised more fuss. It's going to create headache. More crowds. More scrutiny.

JUDAS: What, you want to slow Him down?

JOHN: He's mad at me. He's annoyed I've gotten close to Thomas.

BIG JAMES: I felt that way before we left. I don't care about that now. Tell them what you said. Or do you take it back?

JOHN: No, I still feel it and I'm not afraid to admit it. *(The room is all ears …)* Jesus gave us power but no understanding.

ZEE: Yes.

JOHN: We healed, but still felt overwhelmed.

MATTHEW: I was troubled often.

NATHANAEL: But did He require understanding? It seemed to be more about what we were doing.

BIG JAMES: Easy for you to say. You and Thaddaeus went door to door in Hebron. He's known in Hebron. They probably invited you into their homes.

NATHANAEL *(exchanging a guilty look with Thaddaeus)*: I'll go on harder missions.

JUDAS: Nathanael is right. He never said anything about understanding. And this was temporary anyway.

LITTLE JAMES: Sometimes when I was preaching, I felt like they weren't my words. That I was just … a … channel for His words, nothing of my own.

BIG JAMES: I said things I don't even fully comprehend or live by. I felt like a fraud.

ANDREW: I felt the same way, but it didn't bother me.

EDEN: Instead of arguing about it, you could just ask Jesus about it when He gets back. *(Everyone is taken aback by Eden chiming in. She seems surprised herself.)*

MATTHEW: That's a very good idea.

THADDAEUS: Who can say when that will be?

ALL: Soon.

PHILIP: The most imprecise word.

JOHN: So, some of it was confusing, James. Can you live with that until we get understanding?

Storms

Jesus can and does intervene in life's difficult circumstances—but we still have to face them. Indeed, following doesn't mean Jesus removes us from the storms of life. Instead, He promises to be the solid ground on which we stand, thereby making it possible to endure the wind and rain. Conversely, when we choose the shifting sands of the wide road, stuff falls down and destruction ensues.

The same was true for the disciples. We sometimes think that because they had close physical proximity to Jesus (i.e., they could see Him with their actual eyeballs), they somehow had an easier time of it. We presume, *If only I could see Jesus, if only I could hear His voice, then I'd have the wisdom … the courage … the wherewithal to follow.* But the disciples' experience was the same as ours in that their ability to follow depended on where they placed their hope.

For Bible Nerds (like us) Who Want to Know

Growing up in the home of a crafts-man like Joseph, it was probably quite natural for Jesus to think of construction metaphors. But as Jesus preached about the need for a solid foundation, He also spoke of false prophets.

He said, "Beware of false prophets, who come to you in sheep's clothing but inwardly are ravenous wolves. You will recognize them by their fruits. Are grapes gathered from thornbushes, or figs from thistles? So, every healthy tree bears good fruit, but the diseased tree bears bad fruit. A healthy tree cannot bear bad fruit, nor can a diseased tree bear good fruit. Every tree that does not bear good fruit is cut down and thrown into the fire. Thus you will recognize them by their fruits. Not everyone who says to me, 'Lord, Lord,' will enter the king-dom of heaven" (Matt. 7:15–21).

In Ezekiel 13, God used another con-struction metaphor when address-ing the issue of false prophets. These men were "whitewashing" significant problems in order to cover the sin of the people. But the walls they constructed were cheap and exposed and wouldn't survive the coming storms.

No doubt, it wasn't a coincidence that Jesus's earthly father was a carpenter. So was Jesus. And in some ways, so was His heavenly Father since God constructed the whole wide world and continues to uphold it, in spite of sin's destruc-tive consequences.

Unfortunately, humanity's spiritual real estate tends to fluctuate as often as the weather.

Your Turn

1. Be honest. What makes you feel most secure and steady and stable? In other words, where have you built your metaphorical house?

Rock Beats ~~Scissors~~ Sand

"And everyone who hears these words

of mine and does not do them will

be like a foolish man who built his

house on the sand. And the rain fell,

and the floods came, and the winds

blew and beat against that house, and

it fell, and great was the fall of it."

Matthew 7:26–27

The problem with storms is they're unpredictable (sorry, meteorologists)—you never know how they're going to end. Will the hail leave dents? Will the wind tear off the shingles? Will the tornado come down our street? Will we get sucked into its vortex along with everything else?

And then there are the emotional storms, those that come with a whole different set of questions. Will I lose my job? Will I always be alone? Will I ever be free from addiction? Will the person I love suffer or die? Will I?

We want to know in advance how things are going to end, though we rarely get to.

But that doesn't mean we never get to.

As it turns out, the disciples had similar questions about their lives, about Jesus, and about what their futures would hold (John 13:36–14:11; 21:15–22; Acts 1:6–8). Of course, we now know the answers would've been too difficult to bear since ten of the twelve were eventually martyred because of their allegiance to Christ. Yet, just before raising His friend Lazarus from the dead, Jesus said, "I am the resurrection and the life. Whoever believes in me, though he die, yet shall he live, and everyone who lives and believes in me shall never die" (John 11:25–26).

But despite being miraculously raised from the dead, Lazarus eventually died—which begs the question, what was the point of being raised to life? To give Laz a few more years on our broken, sinful planet? To momentarily spare his sisters the pain they'd eventually experience a second time anyway? Why suspend everyone's suffering when suffering would surely come?

The answer is simple:

To know how the story will end.

Your Turn

2. What storms are you facing?

3. In what ways are you building your house—and your hope—on sand? In what ways are you building on the Rock?

4. When God makes a promise, He keeps it. Circle any or all of the promises below that offer you a surer foundation.

"Have you not known? Have you not heard? The LORD is the everlasting God, the Creator of the ends of the earth. He does not faint or grow weary; his understanding is unsearchable. He gives power to the faint, and to him who has no might he increases strength. Even youths shall faint and be weary, and young men shall fall exhausted; but they who wait for the LORD shall renew their strength; they shall mount up with wings like eagles; they shall run and not be weary; they shall walk and not faint."
Isaiah 40:28–31

"Peace I leave with you; my peace I give to you. Not as the world gives do I give to you. Let not your hearts be troubled, neither let them be afraid."
John 14:27

"And my God will supply every need of yours according to his riches in glory in Christ Jesus. To our God and Father be glory forever and ever. Amen."
Philippians 4:19–20

"His divine power has granted to us all things that pertain to life and godliness, through the knowledge of him who called us to his own glory and excellence, by which he has granted to us his precious and very great promises, so that through them you may become partakers of the divine nature, having escaped from the corruption that is in the world because of sinful desire."

2 Peter 1:3–4

Action Word

"Not everyone who says to me, 'Lord, Lord,' will enter the kingdom of heaven, but the one who does the will of my Father who is in heaven. On that day many will say to me, 'Lord, Lord, did we not prophesy in your name, and cast out demons in your name, and do many mighty works in your name?' And then will I declare to them, 'I never knew you; depart from me, you workers of lawlessness.'"

Matthew 7:21–23

There's an obvious connection between word and deed. We see it in everyday life and complain when a person's behavior doesn't match what he or she claims to believe. Collectively, we're quick to accuse and dismiss a person who seems hypocritical.

We hate that.

For Bible Nerds (like us) Who Want to Know

One of the most common OT Hebrew words translated "believe" (*'āman*), as well as the NT Greek word translated "believe" (*pisteuō*), do not describe mere agreement. Rather, they imply a committed trust.

In English we make this distinction by using an additional word. For example, we recognize the difference between believing that a particular person is the leader of our nation (agreement) and believing in a particular person as the leader of our country (committed trust).

In the NT, James (not the apostle James, but Jesus's younger brother, who eventually became a believer) commented on this important distinction: "You believe that God is one; you do well. Even the demons believe—and shudder!" (James 2:19). And then he called people to true belief—to a committed trust—that shows up in how they live.

James pointed to Abraham in the OT as a prime example (James 2:20–23). As a key model of faith, Abraham did not earn his salvation by believing; rather, his obedience to God demonstrated that his belief was a real, committed trust.

The apostle Paul also pointed to Abraham: "For if Abraham was justified by works, he has something to boast about, but not before God. For what does the Scripture say? 'Abraham believed God, and it was counted to him as righteousness.' Now to the one who works, his wages are not counted as a gift but as his due. And to the one who does not work but believes in him who justifies the ungodly, his faith is counted as righteousness" (Rom. 4:2–5).

So for us, our belief in Jesus Christ as our Savior (Eph. 2:8–9) is made evident by our obedience to Him as Lord (v. 10).

In the same way, agreeing with Jesus's words just isn't enough. After all, He told His chosen ones to hear His words *and do them*. Of course, salvation is based on Jesus's death and resurrection alone: "If you confess with your mouth that Jesus is Lord and believe in your heart that God raised him from the dead, you will be saved" (Rom. 10:9). But believing Jesus means *following* Him, and *following* is a verb—an action word. Meaning, those who believe Jesus do what He says.

Simple enough, right? Our deeds match our words because our hearts are surrendered to the Lord. Except, surrendering gets more difficult when floodwaters rise. Specifically, trusting Jesus when our finances are low or a loved one gets sick goes against our very nature; we prefer to control, wrestle with, and somehow manage that stuff. And yet, following means to surrender control.

We hate that.

So how do we choose to relinquish control and call Jesus "Lord"? How do we ensure our deeds match our words? How do we maintain a posture of faith that doesn't depend on which way (or how hard) the wind is blowing? How do we stand on the Rock of our salvation?

The answer is simple:

We abide.

Hypocrisy:
the practice of claiming to have moral standards or beliefs to which one's own behavior does not conform; pretense.

Surrender:
to submit to the authority of another.

Lord:
someone or something having power, authority, or influence over another; a master or ruler.

"For God alone my soul waits in silence; from him comes my salvation. He alone is my rock and my salvation, my fortress; I shall not be greatly shaken."
Psalm 62:1–2

Your Turn

5. In what ways are you a hypocrite? (Sin causes each one of us to be a hypocrite to some degree, which means literally everyone should be able to answer this question.)

6. Read John 14:6; Ephesians 2:10; and Galatians 2:20–21. In your own words, explain the relationship between being saved by grace alone and doing good works.

7. Reread Matthew 7:24. What does Jesus equate with "building on the rock"? What specific thing can you do today in response to what He said?

Remain

"Abide in me, and I in you. As the branch cannot bear fruit by itself, unless it abides in the vine, neither can you, unless you abide in me.… As the Father has loved me, so have I loved you. Abide in my love. If you keep my commandments, you will abide in my love, just as I have kept my Father's commandments and abide in his love."

John 15:4, 9–10

Abide: to remain stable or fixed in a state; to continue to a place.

The Bible is full of word pictures—metaphors of rock and sand, fruit and vines—because we humans better understand the nature of our invisible God by way of His visible creation. And the meaning of these particular metaphors is the same: Jesus is the source of our strength, the foundation of our hope, and the whole point of Scripture!

We follow Jesus, not because our lives will be storm-free, but because this world isn't all there is. We follow because He has control over death itself, and He has promised to raise us to life in heaven where storms will forevermore be stilled. We follow because, in the meantime, He promises to never leave us or forsake us—to be the solid ground on which we stand.

"Be strong and courageous. Do not fear or be in dread of them, for it is the LORD your God who goes with you. He will not leave you or forsake you."
Deuteronomy 31:6

Indeed, the only way to avoid being tossed by the storms of life is to know and remain in Jesus. To believe His promises and do what He says because the wind and waves obey Him (Matt. 8:27).

And in His power and by His grace, we shall not be moved.

Your Turn

8. Taking a closer look at the vine-and-branch metaphor of John 15, what is a practical way you can choose to abide in Jesus today?

Prayer Focus

Praise Jesus for being your sure foundation, the Rock of your salvation, and your future hope. Thank Him for promising to remain with you in every storm. Ask for more faith to believe His words, and for a greater sense of His peace and presence in the midst of chaos. Pray for the strength to keep following no matter how difficult the circumstances are, knowing that Jesus's way is right and good and true.

Sample Prayer

Dear Jesus,

I am so glad that You have revealed Yourself as the Rock of salvation. Thank You that I don't have to try to save myself; I trust in You. And thank You that, better than any other rock, You are the most sure and unmovable foundation for life and hope. Nevertheless (and as You already know), I am facing storms right now and I'm tempted to try to manage them on my own. Please help me trust You in the midst of these difficulties; please help me experience more of Your peace in this time, even right now. Rather than pulling away from You, I want to remain in You, drawing courage, strength, and hope from You. Please help me do that. By Your Spirit's work in my life, surprise me with some fruit of obedience that comes only from You and not from my own efforts. And I will praise You for it.

Amen.

EXT. COUNTRYSIDE (SPRING, DAY)

(Veronica—i.e., the bleeding woman—is doing laundry when Eden arrives with a tremendous bundle of her own.)

EDEN: Shalom, Veronica.

VERONICA: Your house isn't empty anymore.

EDEN: What?

VERONICA: Those look like men's tunics.

EDEN *(plunging the clothes into the water)*: My husband and his friends returned home.

VERONICA: The perfect place.

EDEN: I assure you, there's nothing perfect about my place—or about me.

VERONICA: I meant Eden. The garden.

EDEN: What brought you here from Caesarea Philippi?

VERONICA: Came to hear the Preacher, on the Mount.

EDEN: Of course.

VERONICA: Surely you were there?

EDEN: Yes! Yes, I … *(distracted by a dark thought)* I was.

VERONICA: What, you didn't like what you heard?

EDEN: I did, it's just that a lot has happened since then. *(changing the subject)* It must have been a hard journey with your … um …

VERONICA: What?

EDEN: Just the—I don't know, your limp.

VERONICA: My limbs are fine. I've been—

(Suddenly both women are uncomfortable, and Veronica is bleeding. She covers the spot. Eden's eyes drift to the mounds of bloody textiles nearby.)

EDEN: How long have you been—

VERONICA: Twelve years.

EDEN: Do you mean days?

VERONICA: I mean years.

EDEN: Twelve!? How is that possible?

VERONICA: It's a rare disease.

EDEN: How have you stayed alive?

VERONICA: It just makes me weak. You better keep your distance. If you touch any of it, you'll be ritually unclean and unable to touch your husband for seven days.

EDEN: Oh, I assure you, I haven't been touching my husband.

(Veronica's eyebrows go up. They wash in silence. After a few more of Eden's glances at the bloody heap, Veronica discloses—)

VERONICA: There's no cure for my ailment. I spent all my money on doctors, and they only made it worse. No hope there.

EDEN: So what do you do with no hope?

VERONICA: I haven't lost *all* hope. There's no cure by doctors. But there could be another way.

"Do not lay up for yourselves treasures on earth, where moth and rust destroy and where thieves break in and steal, but lay up for yourselves treasures in heaven, where neither moth nor rust destroys and where thieves do not break in and steal. For where your treasure is, there your heart will be also."

Matthew 6:19–21

Lesson 5

DELIGHT
in what Jesus delights in

INT. SIMON'S HOME

(Jesus sits with Matthew, Andrew, Little James, and Philip. A few empty wineskins hang nearby. Eden sets a plate before Jesus.)

JESUS: And now, to the breaking of My fast. Thank you, Eden!

EDEN: Of course.

LITTLE JAMES: You fasted while You were away?

JESUS: No, just overnight. Eight hours. *(bites into a cucumber)* Eden! These pickled cucumbers are magnificent!

(Leaning over the sink, Eden purses her lips and chokes back emotion. Matthew sees a concerned but knowing look cross Jesus's face. He says nothing.)

PHILIP: I've been meaning to ask You about fasting.

JESUS: A thing I am very happy not to be doing right now.

PHILIP: John required us to fast at regular intervals, and You've never once asked us to. I mean, there was the time we ate the heads of grain in the wheat field, but we were just hungry. That wasn't intentional fasting.

JESUS: What are you getting at?

PHILIP: The Pharisees fast all the time.

ANDREW: Make a big scene out of it, disfiguring their faces.

PHILIP: If it's such a big deal to them, and they find out we don't do it, don't You think they might, I don't know, weaponize that against us?

JESUS: Can the wedding guests mourn as long as the bridegroom is with them? The days will come when the bridegroom is taken away from them, and then they will fast.

MATTHEW: Taken away?

JESUS *(to Matthew)*: Hold that thought. *(to Philip)* When you fasted before, what did you pray for?

PHILIP: Your arrival.

ANDREW: Right, so what would be the point now?

JESUS: Exactly. Eden, are you fermenting any wine right at the moment?

EDEN *(thrown)*: Uh, yes, in the back room.

JESUS: Little James, please take down that empty wineskin.

PHILIP *(leaning forward)*: Ooh, I feel a lesson coming.

JESUS: Eden, the last time you checked on the wine, what was it doing?

EDEN: What it always does at this stage—sort of bubbling, popping out little plumes of air now and then.

JESUS: James, how does that wineskin feel?

LITTLE JAMES: Stiff. Not very flexible.

JESUS: So if Eden were to put her new wine into that container, what would happen?

PHILIP: The old leather can't stretch anymore.

MATTHEW: The new wine would keep expanding and it would explode.

JESUS: New wine must be put into fresh wineskins.

ANDREW: I'll be the first one to admit I don't get it.

JESUS: The ways of the kingdom I am bringing into this world will not fit in the old containers or frameworks.

PHILIP *(starting to get it)*: Being revolutionary is fun.

Blessings and the Bridegroom

In episode 5 of season 3, we see Jesus's followers experience varying degrees of delight. Zebedee celebrates his newfound interest in olive oil production and includes his talented, business-minded friends. Despite Simon's undefined troubles at home, he and his (unlikely) new friend, Gaius, make progress on a community project. And Jesus returns to His eager disciples, who once again get to bask in His company and otherworldly teaching.

Delight: to take pleasure; to give joy or satisfaction to.

Here's the thing: God intends for all of the above—relationships, new discoveries, teamwork, a job well done, a really good meal, a thriving community, a home to come back to at the end of a long day—to be enjoyed.

Hear that again.

God wants you to enjoy the world He's made because what He's made is good.

"And God saw everything that he had made, and behold, it was very good. And there was evening and there was morning, the sixth day." Genesis 1:31

But even more than earthly blessings, God wants you to enjoy *Him*. To consider your relationship with Him your greatest treasure. To be eager to spend time at His feet, listening to and meditating on His words. To be filled with joy and peace as a result of having been in His presence. To carry His wisdom, love, and grace into your relationships with others. And to have the way you see and experience the world be fundamentally and irrevocably re-formed by the way *He* sees the world.

He wants you to delight in your relationship with the Bridegroom.

Your Turn

1. What are some things in your life—blessings from God—that you really enjoy?

Wineskins

> "No one puts a piece of unshrunk cloth on an old garment, for the patch tears away from the garment, and a worse tear is made. Neither is new wine put into old wineskins. If it is, the skins burst and the wine is spilled and the skins are destroyed. But new wine is put into fresh wineskins, and so both are preserved."
>
> Matthew 9:16–17

To be honest, sometimes practicing religion is easier than pursuing relationship. That is to say, we find strange comfort in leaning on our own behavior instead of on Jesus, and we often view following Him as a set of rules and regulations we have to adhere to—

Religion:
a personal set or institutionalized system of attitudes, beliefs, and practices.

things we must do and the kind of people we must be in order to maintain our good standing with God and others. While it's true that *following* is an action word, and truly knowing Jesus brings repentance and life change, our behavior isn't the endgame.

Relationship:
the state in which two people are connected.

Our relationship with our Creator—with the Bridegroom—is the endgame.

And in Jesus, that's a new thing.

For Bible Nerds (like us) Who Want to Know

In both the Old and New Testaments, the relationship of a bridegroom (modern English = "groom") with his bride is given as a picture of God's relationship to His chosen people.

For example, Isaiah remarks that "as the bridegroom rejoices over the bride, so shall your God rejoice over you" (Isa. 62:5).

Paul compares the love of a husband for his wife to the love that Christ has for His church (Eph. 5:25–29).

Scripture also comments on how unfaithfulness in one's relationship with God brings sorrow in the same way that unfaithfulness in marriage does (e.g., Jer. 2:1–3, 32).

But God faithfully and persistently pursues His people to bring them back into relationship with Him (Hos. 1–3).

In a combination of word pictures, the joy of marriage is even applied to what eternity will be like with God's people inhabiting the new Jerusalem "prepared as a bride adorned for her husband" and introduced as "the Bride, the wife of the Lamb" (Rev. 21:2, 9).

To be clear, relationship with God has always been available by grace through faith (Rom. 4:1–8), but no one has ever been "good" enough to *earn* their own salvation (Gal. 2:16). In Old Testament days, the Israelites had to obey the law of Moses. In return, God promised to lead, protect, and bless them (Deut. 30:15–18; 1 Sam. 12:14–15). But the people couldn't keep the law. So, in order to remain cognizant of the offensiveness of their sin—and because God is holy— they had to make the proper atoning sacrifices.

Over and over and over again.

In this way, the "old covenant" pointed people to their need to trust in God's grace for salvation (Heb. 9:1–10). But it also pointed to the "new covenant"— because what people couldn't accomplish on their own, God would do for them.

And us.

"There is therefore now no condemnation for those who are in Christ Jesus. For the law of the Spirit of life has set you free in Christ Jesus from the law of sin and death. For God has done what the law, weakened by the flesh, could not do. By sending his own Son in the likeness of sinful flesh and for sin, he condemned sin in the flesh, in order that the righteous requirement of the law might be fulfilled in us, who walk not according to the flesh but according to the Spirit" (Rom. 8:1–4).

Jesus ushered in the new covenant and fulfilled the old promise by making *Himself* the ultimate and

"See, I am doing a new thing! Now it springs up; do you not perceive it? I am making a way in the wilderness and streams in the wasteland."
Isaiah 43:19 (NIV)

Grace: unmerited favor of God toward man.

Holy: distinct, set apart, perfect, and untouched by sin.

Atone: to make amends or reparations.

Proper atoning sacrifices for the OT Israelites are described in great detail in the book of Leviticus.

Covenant: a binding agreement.

"Behold, the days are coming, declares the LORD, when I will make a new covenant with the house of Israel and the house of Judah, not like the covenant that I made with their fathers on the day when I took them by the hand to bring them out of the land of Egypt, my covenant that they broke, though I was their husband, declares the LORD. For this is the covenant that I will make with the house of Israel after those days, declares the LORD: I will put my law within them, and I will write it on their hearts. And I will be their God, and they shall be my people."
Jeremiah 31:31–33

perfect sacrifice for sin. And it changed everything! Unfortunately, we sometimes still operate the old way. We're aware of our sin and total inability to be perfect, but we respond by trying to do better in our own strength. *I'll pray more. I'll read my Bible more. I'll call my grandma more.* You get the idea. Add to that our tendency to justify sin by comparing ourselves to others: *At least I'm not as bad as so-and-so.*

What we end up with is more religion … and less relationship.

Jesus used the wineskin metaphor to help His followers understand that He was launching a new thing: a way back into relationship with God as it was intended in the Garden of Eden when everything was blissful and beautiful, joyful and peaceful. To that end, Jesus isn't just another piece of a religious puzzle. He's not a continuation of an old way of life. And He's certainly not a "good" teacher of otherwise common religious practice (think Muhammad, Gandhi, Buddha, whoever).

Jesus, along with the kind of relationship He freely offers, is THE new thing.

And most of us are doing it wrong.

Your Turn

2. What are your religious practices? Meaning, what things do you feel compelled to do *in order* to be "good"?

3. Read Matthew 6:16–18 and explain why the Pharisees' religious practices sometimes got in the way of their relationship with God.

4. Describe your relationship with Jesus. Is it formal or familiar? Is it boring or life-giving? Or (more likely) to what extent is it a mixture of all of the above?

Beasts of Burden

"Come to me, all who labor and are heavy laden, and I will give you rest. Take my yoke upon you, and learn from me, for I am gentle and lowly in heart, and you will find rest for your souls. For my yoke is easy, and my burden is light."

Matthew 11:28–30

Jesus extended a beautiful invitation: to exchange burden for rest. But instead of accepting His offer, it's more common for us to practice religion and hold tightly to our burdens. And life is hard and our struggles are many, which means our loads are heavy. Religion itself can be heavy. But Jesus beckons us to put on *His* yoke. To trade religion for relationship, what is earthly for what is heavenly, what is heavy for what is light. He invites us to believe Him and place our trust in Him.

For Bible Nerds (like us) Who Want to Know

In the largely agrarian first-century world, people would recognize Jesus's reference to a yoke. It was a wooden frame fastened to the neck and shoulders of one or two animals (usually oxen) to get them to work better together (1 Sam. 6:7; 11:7; Luke 14:19). This pairing of working animals was an ancient symbol of subjection of one to another (Gen. 27:40; Lev. 26:13; Deut. 28:48; Jer. 27:1–7; Gal. 5:1; 1 Tim. 6:1).

In Judaism the yoke was a symbol for the OT law. The all-too-typical Pharisaic interpretation of the law was filled with burdensome man-made requirements (Matt. 23:4). But being "yoked" to Jesus—to keep in step with Him and moving in His direction—is not the burdensome way of subjection to human requirements, but rather the restful way of love and faith in Him (1 John 5:1–5).

And here's the kicker: He delights in us when we do.

"He brought me out into a broad place; he rescued
me, because he delighted in me."
Psalm 18:19

"But the LORD takes pleasure in those who
fear him, in those who hope in his steadfast love."
Psalm 147:11

"For the LORD takes delight in his people;
he crowns the humble with victory. Let his faithful people
rejoice in this honor and sing for joy on their beds."
Psalm 149:4–5 (NIV)

"The LORD your God is in your midst, a mighty one who will
save; he will rejoice over you with gladness; he will quiet
you by his love; he will exult over you with loud singing."
Zephaniah 3:17

God delights in His creation, and He delights in your company because He made you! He delights in your acceptance of His forgiveness and grace. He delights in your worship and in your deference to His holiness. He delights in the faith and hope you place in Him. He delights in your participation in His kingdom work.

He delights in you. Though that's not the message religion most often highlights. But oh, how our burdens would be less (not to mention our heavenly treasure would be more) if we delighted in Him too.

Your Turn

5. What burdens are you carrying that Jesus wants to carry?

6. Reread Matthew 11:28–30 and write down the words that describe Jesus and His "yoke."

7. Close your eyes and open your hands to heaven, saying, *"Jesus, I give You _____."* (For example: *"Jesus, I give You the bills I'm not sure how to pay."* Or *"Jesus, I give You my friend … my child … my spouse."* Or *"Jesus, I give You my broken heart."* Or *"Jesus, I give You the burdens too great for me to bear."*)

Time to Delight

"Delight yourself in the LORD, and he

will give you the desires of your heart."

Psalm 37:4

Remember, *believe* is an action word; it reveals itself in our behavior.

We believe Jesus, so we're loving, even when the people around us aren't. We believe, so we lay up treasure in heaven by being generous on earth. We believe, so we spend our time

For Bible Nerds (like us) Who Want to Know

The idea of rejoicing at the right time in the things God has provided recalls the poetic OT saying in Ecclesiastes 3:1–8. There the author (sometimes called "The Preacher") writes about a time for everything, including "a time to weep, and a time to laugh; a time to mourn, and a time to dance" (v. 4—perhaps you can hear these words to the tune of the song "Turn! Turn! Turn!" made famous by the Byrds).

The Preacher of the Old Testament thought about delighting in the things God provided at the correct time. "For everything there is a season, and a time for every matter under heaven: a time to be born, and a time to die; a time to plant, and a time to pluck up what is planted; a time to kill, and a time to heal; a time to break down, and a time to build up; a time to weep, and a time to laugh; a time to mourn, and a time to dance" (Eccl. 3:1–4).

And now Jesus, the Preacher of the New Testament, is likewise calling His followers to live out God's priorities to delight. "Then the disciples of John came to him, saying, 'Why do we and the Pharisees fast, but your disciples do not fast?' And Jesus said to them, 'Can the wedding guests mourn as long as the bridegroom is with them? The days will come when the bridegroom is taken away from them, and then they will fast'" (Matt. 9:14–15).

building God's kingdom and telling others to come and see. We believe, so we trade our strife and struggle for the rest we so desperately need.

We believe, so we delight in the One who delights in us.

As we discussed in the previous lesson, while our choices can't earn our place in heaven, obeying Jesus certainly benefits us here on earth. After all, experiencing God's delight in an otherwise dark and messed-up world is definitely a benefit. When we delight ourselves in the Lord—when we talk to Him, read His Word, worship, and tell others about Him—not only are our burdens eased, but the very desires of our hearts are satisfied. Because, as divine planning would have it, a relationship with the Lord *is* the deepest desire of every human heart.

Religion is heavy and impossible to maintain. Relationship with Jesus, on the other hand, is light because (a) He carries our burdens, (b) He transforms our hearts to be more like His, and (c) He delights in us as we delight in Him.

Your Turn

8. Give God cause for delight right now. Close your eyes and open your hands to heaven, saying, *"Jesus, You are _____."* (*"Jesus, You are gracious. Jesus, You are merciful. Jesus, You are Lord. Jesus, You are all-powerful and perfect in every way ..."*)

Prayer Focus

Jesus, You are gracious. Jesus, You are merciful. Jesus, You are Lord. Jesus, You are all-powerful and perfect in every way ... (See what we did there?)

EXT. SEA OF GALILEE
(Veronica—the no-longer-bleeding-because-Jesus-healed-her woman—floats on her back in the glimmering water.)

JESUS: You there!

(Startled, Veronica bolts upright as she's called. A beat, and then she recognizes Jesus and His disciples entering the water.)

VERONICA: Oh no! Did I make You unclean? Did the priest send You?

JESUS: He thinks he did. We just wanted to go for a swim.

SIMON: Joke's on him.

MARY MAGDALENE: We wanted to find you.

JESUS: To see how you're doing.

> **Sample Prayer**
>
> Lord Jesus,
>
> You are such an awesome, selfless, loving, merciful, kind, generous, patient, perfect, powerful Savior. You are worthy of worship for who You are. And You have given me so many good things! Salvation from sin and the hope of eternity with You are bigger than I sometimes grasp. But even here, in the midst of my struggles, I recognize that I have many, many delights. My home, clothing, and food. My history and skills, my job and my hobbies. My family and friends, neighbors and coworkers. And, of course, Your Spirit within me. You are worthy of praise and thanks for all these things—they are gifts from You. Thank You.
>
> Amen.

VERONICA: Thank You! I-I know I disturbed You …

JESUS: It was a welcome disturbance. My favorite kind.

(Jesus looks at Simon, John, and Big James. Big James shoves John down into the water by both shoulders. Lots of laughter. Simon soon joins the fray. John comes up, fights back.)

JESUS (to Veronica): If you'll excuse Me, I can't miss this.

(Jesus turns and strokes His way into the splashing. Thaddaeus and Philip and others now fully in. The women press in close to Veronica.)

TAMAR: Twelve years … How did you survive?

VERONICA: It's a long story.

MARY MAGDALENE: Good stories usually are.

(Camera slowly pulls back from the group of disciples with Jesus. Most are swimming, but Jesus and Big James have Thaddaeus and Philip on their shoulders for a chicken fight. Laughter and splashing ensues as we—CUT TO BLACK.)

"Ask, and it will be given to you; seek, and you will find; knock, and it will be opened to you. For everyone who asks receives, and the one who seeks finds, and to the one who knocks it will be opened."

Matthew 7:7–8

Lesson 6

ASK
because Jesus tells you to

EXT. TENT CITY

(Jesus is healing the masses when He notices a mute man with a chalkboard hung around his neck with twine. He is writing Hebrew on it desperately; his friend tries to translate quickly for Jesus. Jesus says to him—)

JESUS: I know.

(Jesus gestures to Nathanael for his knife. Nathanael hands his blade over. Jesus slices the rope from around the man's neck. The chalkboard falls with a clank. Before the man or his friend can react, Jesus places His hands on the man's neck. Former mute chews his tongue, stretches it, opens his mouth wide. Simon and the boys arrive close enough to hear.)

FORMER MUTE: I've never said anything with my own voice.

JESUS: Where would you like to start?

FORMER MUTE *(clutching Jesus's tunic—)*: Blessed are You, Lord Our God, King of the Universe …

JESUS *(pulling the man close—)*: Let's save those big titles for a little later.

SIMON: Master.

JESUS *(turning to Simon)*: Yes. Who do we have here?

JOHN: These are two of Your cousin's disciples, Avner and Nadab.

AVNER: Jesus of Nazareth.

JESUS (*turning back to the former mute*): *That* name I respond to readily, though I'll not be returning to Nazareth in this lifetime.

SIMON: The Baptizer has an urgent question for You.

JESUS: I recognize you from the day John introduced me to Andrew.

NADAB: "Behold the Lamb of God who takes away the sin of the world."

JESUS: Yes, good memory. My cousin can get excited. What does John want to know?

AVNER: Simon brought us in haste. This isn't appropriate here; we can talk later.

JESUS: Simon?

SIMON: I actually think now's the perfect time.

JESUS (*looking at the crowd*): Who of you has experienced John the Baptizer in some way? (*Many nod, raise their hands, say "me."*) I know some of you rejected John, but some of you believed his message. He has had a profound impact on so many in this region, and these are two of his disciples; let's welcome them.

(*A smattering of clapping and encouragement. Avner and Nadab look more nervous. Simon looks pleased at the building tension.*)

JESUS (CONT'D): Some of you may know that John is currently imprisoned by Herod in Machaerus. I think it'd be very instructive for us to hear what is on his mind in the midst of such challenge.

AVNER (*hesitant*): It's a difficult question, it might be better privately.

JESUS (*quietly, to Avner*): It's fine. This is healthy.

AVNER: He sent us to ask You … are You really the One who is to come … (*even quieter*) Or should we look for someone else?

JESUS: Say that last part again?

NADAB: Should we look for someone else?

JESUS: For those who couldn't hear … John the Baptizer, my cousin who has prepared the way for Me, is questioning if I'm the Messiah. Or if maybe we should keep waiting. (*turning to John's disciples—*) John is getting impatient, yes? It's one of his quirks.

NADAB: He didn't give details, just sent us with the question.

JESUS: Hmm.

AVNER: He … has been in prison a long time.

NADAB: Word reached our ears about what happened in Nazareth. That You said the Spirit of the Lord is upon You to proclaim liberty to the captives.

AVNER: If You say You're here to free prisoners, then why does he remain? He rightfully wonders why You would allow his entire ministry to be halted by an impostor king.

JESUS: Proclaiming liberty to the captives can mean more than just freeing inmates. There are many kinds of captivity that keep people.

NADAB: Is that what we're supposed to tell him?

JESUS: No, that's just for you.

AVNER: We heard our former comrades Andrew and Philip have gone to the Decapolis. Is that where You're planning to launch the revolution to overthrow Rome?

JESUS: I have something in mind for the Decapolis, and it will be revolutionary, but probably not in the way you're thinking.

NADAB (growing impatient): What are we supposed to report back?

JESUS: Go and tell John what you hear and see: the blind receive their sight, the lame walk, the lepers are cleansed, the mute speak, and the poor have good news preached to them.

Expectations

When Jesus came on the scene in the tumultuous time of the first-century Mediterranean world, He wasn't exactly what people were looking for. Many of the Israelites expected their promised Messiah to be a strong and mighty deliverer of the Jews, the One whom the nation of Israel believed would rescue them from the Roman occupation and reestablish them in their homeland.

But as we discussed in lesson 3, not only was Jesus plain and poor, overlooked and unesteemed, He was often misunderstood. Even those who followed Him didn't have Him totally figured out because some of the things He said were veiled and confusing. In addition, some of His behaviors were surprising and different from any other teacher or Jewish leader who'd come before Him.

"The beginning of the gospel of Jesus Christ, the Son of God. As it is written in Isaiah the prophet, 'Behold, I send my messenger before your face, who will prepare your way, the voice of one crying in the wilderness: "Prepare the way of the Lord, make his paths straight,"' John appeared, baptizing in the wilderness and proclaiming a baptism of repentance for the forgiveness of sins. And all the country of Judea and all Jerusalem were going out to him and were being baptized by him in the river Jordan, confessing their sins."
Mark 1:1–5

Bottom line: Jesus didn't fit into preconceived notions, and it brought questions to the minds of His disciples—including the wholly devoted "Preparer of the Way," John the Baptizer.

John had already identified Jesus as "the Lamb of God, who takes away the sin of the world" (John 1:29), and he'd been admonishing people to follow Jesus rather than himself (John 3:30). But now this radical wilderness preacher was stuck in a prison cell, which wasn't what he'd envisioned for himself or the movement he'd started, especially if the Messiah was at hand.

And, suddenly, that was a big *if.*

Your Turn

1. What expectations do you have of Jesus and of what following Him is supposed to be like?

Even the Baptizer

"Now when John heard in prison about the deeds of the
Christ, he sent word by his disciples and said to him, 'Are you
the one who is to come, or shall we look for another?'"

Matthew 11:2–3

John the Baptist had been proclaiming the coming Messiah—it was the God-given purpose of his miraculously conceived life (Luke 1:5–13). He preached with complete abandon, spreading his "repent and be ready" message despite all the social and religious alienation that came with it. He was all-in. He lived off the land (ate bugs), wore it on his back (camel hair), and preached to anyone who would listen. And then he baptized Jesus and witnessed *"the heavens [opening], and he saw the Spirit of God descending like a dove and coming to rest on [Jesus]; and behold, a voice from heaven said, 'This is my beloved Son, with whom I am well pleased'"* (Matt. 3:16–17).

As if that weren't enough, then came the miracles. Jesus was gathering followers and moving from town to town, preaching and healing and astonishing the crowds. And all the while John was fulfilling his mission, telling people to repent and pointing them to Jesus. Even as the crowds around John got smaller, he was zealous in his faith and unmovable in his convictions. "I am not the Christ, but I have been sent before him … Therefore this joy of mine is now complete. [Jesus] must increase, but I must decrease" (John 3:28–30).

John was faith-filled.

That is, until he landed in prison.

John quickly discovered that unmet expectations can be totally derailing. Because in spite of all the miraculous things he'd witnessed, and in spite of himself being an actual fulfillment of Old Testament prophecy (Isa. 40:3), John wasn't immune to fear or frustration. On the contrary, his circumstances were confusing and discouraging, even terrifying—and he wavered. In this jail-cell moment, he probably felt abandoned by the

One he'd devoted his life to. From all accounts, it appears Jesus didn't even visit His faithful servant-cousin in prison.

And questions loomed.

Your Turn

2. Highlight John 3:28–30 in your Bible and explain in the space below what you think those verses mean.

3. "For everyone who asks receives, and the one who seeks finds, and to the one who knocks it will be opened." In light of Matthew 7:8, explain why John's question for Jesus was awesome and exactly the right way to handle his jailhouse doubt.

4. What looming questions do you have right now? What fear or confusion do you need to take to Jesus?

Asked and Answered

"Jesus answered them, 'Go and tell John what
you hear and see: the blind receive their sight
and the lame walk, lepers are cleansed and the
deaf hear, and the dead are raised up, and the
poor have good news preached to them. And
blessed is the one who is not offended by me.'"

Matthew 11:4–6

Jesus wasn't upset with John. He wasn't incredulous that John was having a moment—quite the opposite. He responded to John's doubt in two parts: (1) remember what you know about Me; and (2) dig deep and trust Me. In other words, "Don't let this moment derail you, My good and faithful servant. I AM who I say I AM, even when your expectations go unmet." And then Jesus turned back to the crowd and publicly honored John's faith: "Truly I tell you, among those born of women there has not risen anyone greater than John the Baptist" (Matt. 11:11 NIV).

Jesus knows how hard unmet expectations can be—which is why He encourages us to ask! He wants us to bring to Him our doubts, confusion, and fear along with all of the questions they unearth: "Which of you, if your son asks for bread, will give him a stone? Or if he asks for a fish, will give him a snake? If you, then, though you are evil, know how to give good gifts to your children, how much more will your Father in heaven give good gifts to those who ask him!" (Matt. 7:9–11 NIV).

For Bible Nerds (like us) Who Want to Know

After Jesus told the crowd, "There has not risen anyone greater than John the Baptist," He went on to say, "Yet the one who is least in the kingdom of God is greater than he" (Luke 7:28).

Who was He referring to?

Well, us.

The key to understanding this verse lies in simply recognizing where we are in history. John the Baptist was the last of the Old Testament–style prophets with forward-looking faith about the coming Messiah. He got to meet Jesus and interact with Him, but John died before the death and resurrection of Jesus.

Those of us who have come after John have the great privilege of backward-looking faith at the victorious work of Jesus and the launch of the kingdom of God with the resurrection. And now we get to share the gospel with a fuller understanding than even John the Baptizer had.

For Bible Nerds (like us) Who Want to Know

Jesus compares God's way of giving to the way good parents give to their children. No stone or serpents in place of food—good parents provide for their kids. Good parents respond to their children's needs in love, action, wisdom, and grace.

It's also of note that good parents don't give serpents, even when kids ask for them—and sometimes kids ask for them. Like children, we often want things that aren't in our best interest. It's the job of loving, engaged parents to say "no" or "not yet" as often as they say "yes" because we've all seen the social media posts, news segments, and daytime talk shows displaying the consequences of parents saying "yes" too often.

Which means it's fair to say that our perfect heavenly Father doesn't and shouldn't say "yes" to everything we ask.

Of course, that doesn't mean God always responds the way we (with our limited understanding) want Him to. He's certainly not held hostage by our doubt or disappointment, as though He has to prove Himself—the miracles (including Jesus's death and resurrection) have already done that. And so, our asks don't determine God's answers. As we mentioned, Jesus didn't visit John in prison, and He didn't get him out. And then John was executed (Matt. 14:1–12; Mark 6:14–29).

But here's the beautiful thing: the moment after he lost his life, the Baptizer was in heaven where his faith became sight and his ears heard the words "Well done, My good and faithful servant."

And all the earthly expectations he ever had were far surpassed.

Your Turn

5. Read Jeremiah 29:11; Proverbs 3:5–6; and Hebrews 12:11. How might these verses impact any confusion and fear you may feel when you're waiting on God for answers?

6. While it's true that God doesn't always answer the way we want Him to, what does James 1:5 tell us we'll *always* get when we ask for it?

7. Read Matthew 7:7–11 again. Instead of focusing on what you want, what do these verses reveal about God's character as well as His heart toward you?

"Ask, and it will be given to you; seek, and you will find; knock, and it will be opened to you. For everyone who asks receives, and the one who seeks finds, and to the one who knocks it will be opened. Or which one of you, if his son asks him for bread, will give him a stone? Or if he asks for a fish, will give him a serpent? If you then, who are evil, know how to give good gifts to your children, how much more will your Father who is in heaven give good things to those who ask him!"
Matthew 7:7–11

Nitty-Gritty

"And this is the confidence that we have toward

him, that if we ask anything according to his

will he hears us. And if we know that he hears

us in whatever we ask, we know that we have

the requests that we have asked of him."

1 John 5:14–15

Scripture context matters, which is why most of us don't own a mansion. And 1 John provides us some context, as well as a key ingredient for asking:

Ask according to God's will.

In other words, God is not subject to our whims. He's not a genie in a bottle, waiting patiently to grant us wishes. On the contrary. He's the Alpha and Omega, Creator and Controller, Redeemer and Restorer. He's the all-powerful, all-knowing, all-seeing King of the Universe. His understanding is beyond measure (Ps. 147:5). His thoughts are not our thoughts, neither are His ways our ways (Isa. 55:6–9), but His plans *are* both for good (Jer. 29:11–13) and for His glory (Rom. 8:28).

Alpha and Omega: the beginning and the end; the first and last letters of the Greek alphabet, used to designate the comprehensiveness of God.

And we have access to Him.

And He's telling us to ask.

So, like the Baptizer, we bring the nitty-gritty of our hearts and lives to the Lord—including our confusion, doubt, and fear—because He knows everything and can do anything, and because we can trust Him to handle our questions with care, kindness, patience, and truth. In His perfect wisdom and abounding love, He'll do everything we ask that aligns with His perfect will.

Your Turn

8. Write down a list of God's attributes that correlate with your circumstances, and ask Him to bring His resources to bear on whatever you're dealing with. (For example: Are you fearful? God is powerful, omniscient, and always available. Are you confused? God is wise, sovereign, and faithful. Are you discouraged? God is all-loving, ever-present, and unsurpassable.)

Prayer Focus

Thank God for inviting you to bring your questions to Him. Praise Him for promising to respond when you do. Ask your heavenly Father to grow your faith, enabling you to come to Him first and to accept His answers.

Sample Prayer

Dear Lord,

Thank You that You are not afraid of my questions and fears and doubts. Forgive me for the times I've tried to lean on my own wisdom, courage, and confidence when I should've been turning to You. Thank You that You've invited me to bring my problems and questions to You. And thank You for the encouragement of Your response to John the Baptist. Please help me look to Scripture for the answers You've already provided, and help me trust You for the answers I'm still waiting for. Please grant me the patient faith I need to accept what You say as loving, trustworthy, and true.

Amen.

EXT. CAPERNAUM SIDE STREET (DUSK, OR NIGHT)

(Simon, James, John, and Jesus turn a corner into a quiet side street.)

SIMON: I can never decide what is more fun … watching You do miracles or watching the reactions.

JOHN: The miracles are better when Pharisees are around. *(Big James steps ahead and indicates for everyone to stop.)*

BIG JAMES: All right, we need to get You to a new place … Do You have a camp we should take You to, or do You want to stay at Simon's again? Probably best if it's a new place, maybe with Andrew, I think it'd be—

(They all notice and turn toward Barnaby and Shula as they emerge from an alley. They approach slowly, Shula's hand on Barnaby's shoulder. Jesus and the others stare a moment. Barnaby takes a deep breath and, while staring at Jesus, indicates his hand toward Shula. Jesus gives an empathetic look. He knows what this is about.)

SHULA *(to Barnaby)*: Who is it? Why did we stop?

BARNABY: It's Him.

SHULA *(embarrassed)*: Barnaby, we don't need—

JESUS: Shula, it's fine. Thank you for bringing Barnaby here for a healing of his leg. *(Shula chuckles.)*

BARNABY: No, I brought her here, she's the one who—

JESUS: I know, Barnaby.

BARNABY: Ah … ha. Of course *(indicating to Shula)*, please … she won't ask.

JESUS: Shula, are you afraid to ask for healing?

SHULA *(lowering her head)*: Yes.

JESUS: Do you have faith I can heal you?

SHULA: Of course.

JESUS: Then why haven't you asked?

SHULA: You have so much to do, so many people who need You more. I am used to this.

JESUS: Shula, look up.

SHULA *(chuckling)*: Look up? I can't see You anyway.

JESUS: I want to see you. *(She lifts her head.)* You and Barnaby have been so kind and lovely since I first met you. You've had such strong faith even though you haven't seen a miracle.

SHULA *(emotional now—)*: You redeemed my friend. Mary's miracle was so clear to me I didn't need sight.

JESUS: I know. You see better than most in this region. But … since your friend Barnaby here won't leave Me alone …

(He winks at Barnaby, and not for the first time. Jesus lifts His left hand to Shula's eyes, His right hand behind her neck. Barnaby raises his eyebrows excitedly. As Jesus looks to the sky, He presses His hand against her eyes, and she gasps. He pulls His hands away, and her eyes are closed tight. She puts her hands over her eyes and starts to cry. Barnaby leans in.)

BARNABY: Well?! Did it work?

SHULA: It's been so long I'm afraid to look.

JESUS *(lowering her hands …)*: It's time, Shula.

"If you love those who love you, what benefit is that to you? For even sinners love those who love them. And if you do good to those who do good to you, what benefit is that to you? For even sinners do the same. And if you lend to those from whom you expect to receive, what credit is that to you? Even sinners lend to sinners, to get back the same amount. But love your enemies, and do good, and lend, expecting nothing in return, and your reward will be great, and you will be sons of the Most High, for he is kind to the ungrateful and the evil. Be merciful, even as your Father is merciful."

Luke 6:32–36

Lesson 7

WELCOME
who Jesus welcomes

INT. ANDREW'S FLAT (NIGHT)

(Judas is packing little satchels of pita slices and dates when Andrew and Philip come tumbling through the door.)

JUDAS: Welcome back!

PHILIP: At least ONE person is happy to see us.

ANDREW *(off Judas's confusion)*: He's a different Philip right now.

PHILIP: For good reason!

ANDREW: Judas, quickly, boil some water. *(noticing little bags)* What are these?

JUDAS: Oh, I was making packages of food for the homeless. Little James said it's a Purim tradition.

ANDREW: Purim! I had completely forgotten.

PHILIP: How can we celebrate a holiday in this moment??

JUDAS: What do you mean? What happened in the Decapolis?

PHILIP: We made a mess. Our teaching—

ANDREW: We did NOT intentionally create a mess. We preached the words of our Rabbi and some people … took issue. Where's the vinegar?

JUDAS: Oh—it's on the bottom shelf. I rearranged the bottles. The way you had them organized was very inefficient.

PHILIP: The Decapolis is in full-scale meltdown and you're rearranging cabinets?

ANDREW: Philip, you're supposed to be the stable one in our group, what's gotten into you? How could he have known?

JUDAS: Why do you need vinegar?

ANDREW: To disinfect the wound.

PHILIP: So it doesn't spread through my mortal body and kill me?

ANDREW: Actually, yes! *(Andrew pours vinegar onto the wound and Philip howls.)*

JUDAS: You still haven't told me what you did to the Decapolis.

ANDREW: Not what we did.

PHILIP: What we SAID.

JUDAS: To smooth things over?

ANDREW: Sometimes people respond better to stories than to teaching, so …

JUDAS: A parable! Oh good! Which one?

ANDREW: The Banquet. PHILIP: Banquet parable.

JUDAS: I love a banquet.

PHILIP: We might as well tell him.

JUDAS: Yeah, I'd love to hear it.

ANDREW: Thank you, Philip. Judas … it comes directly from Jesus. So, it is perfect … don't misunderstand.

JUDAS: Okay. But what?

ANDREW: I think perhaps Jesus shares it when He wants a challenge.

JUDAS: Were you challenged?

ANDREW *(too fast—)*: Oh yes.

PHILIP: You could say challenged. Challenged is fair.

ANDREW: So, it goes like this: One time there was a rich man who was throwing a big party.

PHILIP: A great banquet that he wanted lots of people to come to.

ANDREW: And so, he sent his servant to those invited, saying, "Come! Everything is ready. It's time."

PHILIP: But all of them made excuses. The first said, "I have bought a field, and I need to go out and look it over. Please excuse me."

ANDREW: And another said, "I have bought five yokes of oxen, and I must go to examine them. I can't come." Another said, "I have married a wife, and therefore I cannot come."

JUDAS: Those are perfectly legitimate reasons.

ANDREW *(to Philip)*: Even our own people heckle.

PHILIP: Someone in the crowd said exactly the same thing.

ANDREW: So, the servant came and reported these things to his master. The master of the house became angry, so he said to the servant, "Go out quickly to the streets of the city and bring in the poor and crippled and blind and lame."

PHILIP: So, he did that, and they came, but even then there was still room left over at the banquet. And the Master said, "Go out to the highways and hedges and compel people to come in, that my house may be filled." *(Judas shifts uncomfortably.)*

JUDAS: You said this to a mixed crowd.

ANDREW: We did not know the extent to which the crowd was mixed.

JUDAS: So, "go out and find some leftovers" did not exactly play well.

ANDREW: It should have. God wants everyone to come to the party!

PHILIP: The Master said, "I want My WHOLE HOUSE filled!" Everyone's invited!

JUDAS: So, tell me if I have this right. The Jews understood you to mean that Jesus was calling for Gentiles, and the Gentiles thought you were calling them second-class. And then the conservatives who live by Jeremiah would have heard you saying the original guests who didn't want to attend the banquet would miss the party. And those better versed in Isaiah, "Behold, I am doing a new thing," were probably emboldened, except that Gentiles were there.

(A pause. Philip and Andrew look at each other, then back to Judas.)

ANDREW: Yeah, that's about right.

Troublemaker

Jesus doesn't have a litmus test for who He welcomes. In fact, His unique and unfettered interactions with others were a constant source of conflict during His three-year ministry.

Because the Israelites were not nearly as welcoming.

Incidentally, neither are we. But let's not get ahead of ourselves.

In episode 7 of season 3, we once again see the people around Jesus trying to make sense of Him. Is He a preacher, teacher, or healer? Is He a rabble-rouser, political instigator, or rebel revolutionary? Is He a community organizer, a philanthropist, or just an all-around nice guy?

"There is neither Jew nor Greek, there is neither slave nor free, there is no male and female, for you are all one in Christ Jesus."
Galatians 3:28

People in the first century tried to come up with a category for Jesus—and we've been doing it ever since. Many answers to the question of His identity have been circulated throughout the years, especially since Jesus associated with every kind of person: religious and nonreligious, rich and poor, young and old, men and women, Jews and non-Jews.

He doesn't turn anyone away.

So who is Jesus, *really*? And what does His behavior toward people reveal about His character? And what does His character teach His followers about their own?

Well, a lot, actually.

Your Turn

1. Let's get real, real fast. Who do you struggle to welcome?

The Invitation

"A man once gave a great banquet and invited many. And at the
time for the banquet he sent his servant to say to those who had
been invited, 'Come, for everything is now ready.' But they all
alike began to make excuses. The first said to him, 'I have bought
a field, and I must go out and see it. Please have me excused.'
And another said, 'I have bought five yoke of oxen, and I go to
examine them. Please have me excused.' And another said, 'I have
married a wife, and therefore I cannot come.' So the servant came
and reported these things to his master. Then the master of the
house became angry and said to his servant, 'Go out quickly to
the streets and lanes of the city, and bring in the poor and crippled
and blind and lame.… Go out to the highways and hedges and
compel people to come in, that my house may be filled.'"

Luke 14:16–23

Jesus's parable in the Gospel of Luke (also told in Matt. 22:1–14) upset some of
His listeners. And that's an understatement since they, in fact, wanted to kill Him for
implying God's salvation—His "welcome"—extended beyond the nation of Israel:
"Then the Pharisees went and plotted how to entangle him in his words" (Matt. 22:15).
Returning injury for their insult, and because they were rejecting Jesus, the Master would
give them exactly what they wanted: *He* would reject *them*: "For I tell you, none of those
men who were invited shall taste my banquet" (Luke 14:24).

The whole thing was completely countercultural for those who expected salvation to
be offered only to the Jews—which was a common misconception. Many people confused
the Old Testament message that salvation would come through the Jews
with the idea that salvation would come only to the Jews.

"If you confess with your mouth that Jesus is Lord and believe in your heart that God raised him from the dead, you will be saved. For with the heart one believes and is justified, and with the mouth one confesses and is saved. For the Scripture says, 'Everyone who believes in him will not be put to shame.' For there is no distinction between Jew and Greek; for the same Lord is Lord of all, bestowing his riches on all who call on him. For 'everyone who calls on the name of the Lord will be saved.'"
Romans 10:9–13

"For the grace of God has appeared, bringing salvation for all people."
Titus 2:11

"The Lord is not slow to fulfill his promise as some count slowness, but is patient toward you, not wishing that any should perish, but that all should reach repentance."
2 Peter 3:9

Conditional:
subject to one or more requirements being met; made or granted on certain terms.

That's a big difference, obviously. But as it turns out, God's invitation is far more inclusive than most people expect it to be. Indeed, *all* who accept Jesus's offer of forgiveness and eternal life are welcome because God is in the process of filling His heavenly banquet table! The only requirement to attend is to accept His free invitation.

Yet, like the Israelites, we often judge people and consider them unworthy. We stare when they look, act, or speak differently than we're used to. We draw strong denominational distinctions, and then we add our church doctrine to Jesus's salvation banquet criteria. We rank sins as though some are worse than others when the truth is we "all have sinned and fall short of the glory of God" (Rom. 3:23).

As a result, our welcome becomes conditional.

And that has to change.

Your Turn

2. In what ways have you felt welcomed by Jesus?

3. In what ways have you felt unwelcomed by Jesus's followers?

4. Chosen people have had their lives changed by Jesus and seek to be like Him. According to Matthew 5:43–48, what does that mean when it comes to interacting with those who *don't* believe in Him?

Welcome Them, Welcome Me

"'For I was hungry and you gave me food, I was thirsty and you gave me drink, I was a stranger and you welcomed me, I was naked and you clothed me, I was sick and you visited me, I was in prison and you came to me.' Then the righteous will answer him, saying, 'Lord, when did we see you hungry and feed you, or thirsty and give you drink? And when did we see you a stranger and welcome you, or naked

For Bible Nerds (like us) Who Want to Know

Speaking of banquets, in this episode, the people are celebrating the festival of Purim: a day set aside every year commemorating the salvation of the Jews from Haman's plot to kill all those who were living in exile in Persia in 356 BC.

The book of Esther recounts how the festival of Purim came into being, and the "jolly holiday" celebrates how the Jewish people narrowly escaped annihilation, thanks to the bravery of Esther and Mordecai.

Interestingly, while God is everywhere present in the story of Esther, the book itself is one of two in the Bible that doesn't actually mention God—the other being Song of Solomon.

and clothe you? And when did we see you sick or in prison and visit you?' And the King will answer them, 'Truly, I say to you, as you did it to one of the least of these my brothers, you did it to me.'"

Matthew 25:35–40

Jesus wants His followers to be tolerant of others. More than that—He wants us to be gracious and kind and patient. He wants us to be loving and generous and attentive to people's needs. He wants us to be concerned enough to pray for those who are struggling, and to welcome and even serve them.

> "You have heard that it was said, 'You shall love your neighbor and hate your enemy.' But I say to you, Love your enemies and pray for those who persecute you, so that you may be sons of your Father who is in heaven. For he makes his sun rise on the evil and on the good, and sends rain on the just and on the unjust. For if you love those who love you, what reward do you have? Do not even the tax collectors do the same? And if you greet only your brothers, what more are you doing than others? Do not even the Gentiles do the same? You therefore must be perfect, as your heavenly Father is perfect."
> Matthew 5:43–48

When we do, He counts it for Himself!

"Truly, I say to you … you did it to me."

What more motivation do we need than to serve our Master, Lord, and Savior? The One who loved us while we were still sinners (Rom. 5:8). The One who took our sins upon Himself (1 Pet. 2:24) so that we could be with Him forever in heaven where the celebrating will never cease (Rev. 21:1–4). The One who required nothing of us but our willingness to accept His free gift of salvation (Eph. 2:8–9). The One who continues to be patient with us as we work out that salvation (Phil. 2:12–13), faithfully and mercifully making us more like Him every day (2 Cor. 3:16–18).

We welcome others because He welcomed us.

And we love Him for it.

"Beloved, let us love one another, for love is from God, and whoever loves has been born of God and knows God.… We love because he first loved us" (1 John 4:7, 19).

Your Turn

5. "But I say to you, Love your enemies and pray for those who persecute you, <u>so that</u> you may be sons [and daughters] of your Father in heaven." Explain why loving *even your enemies* makes you a son or daughter of God.

6. When speaking about "the least of these my brothers" (Matt. 25:35–40), what change does Jesus encourage His followers to make in the way we view our interactions with others?

> In the NT era, the plural Greek term for "brothers" (*adelphoi*) was regularly used to include men and women in a familial metaphor, thus meaning "brothers and sisters."

7. Write down the name of someone God is putting on your heart to welcome today.

Caveat

"If the world hates you, know that it has hated me before it hated you. If you were of the world, the world would love you as its own; but because you are not of the world, but I chose you out of the world, therefore the world hates you."

John 15:18–19

Our welcome of other people—our treatment of them and the way we respond to them—is supposed to be independent of their attitudes and actions toward us. And unfortunately, Jesus promised that we'd be hated just like He was.

Hate is a strong word. But thanks be to God that He's not asking us to welcome others in our own strength! When we surrender our lives to the Lord, (a) the Holy Spirit indwells our hearts, enabling us to treat others the way God does, with patience, mercy, and grace; and (b) He works in and through us to gather more people to Himself—which means He uses us to build His heavenly kingdom, graciously making us an integral part of His grand plan to redeem and restore the whole of creation.

When you struggle to welcome someone, start with prayer: "Love your enemies and pray for those who persecute you" (Matt. 5:44).

And it starts with our welcome.

Your Turn

8. Let's finish where we started: Who is Jesus, *really*? And what does His behavior toward people reveal about His character? And what does His character teach His followers about their own?

Prayer Focus

Praise God for welcoming you, just as you are. Thank Him for forgiving you and restoring you, for never leaving or forsaking you, and for faithfully making you more like Jesus. Ask Him for an overflow of His love to be poured out on the people around you who need it. Pray for strength, courage, and humility to welcome others the way your Savior does.

Sample Prayer

Dear Master in heaven,

Thank You for my salvation by faith alone in Jesus. Thank You for welcoming me into Your kingdom, into Your family, and to Your banquet in eternity (Rev. 19:1–10). Forgive me for the times I fall into pride, acting like I somehow deserve to treat others like I'm better than them. Thank You that Your presence is always part of my life even now by Your Spirit (Rom. 8:9–11). And by Your Spirit, please raise up within me a Christlike love that welcomes others. May I respond lovingly to the needs of those around me, even with the strength to love those who are my enemies, so that they too might come to faith in You.

Amen.

INT. ANDREW'S FLAT

(The disciples are crammed into Andrew's tiny apartment. Cups of water and meager plates of bread are passed. They have just filled Jesus in on the predicament in Decapolis.)

JESUS: And what was your strategy to clarify it?

PHILIP: We told, or we … *(Philip and Andrew exchange a nervous look.)*

ANDREW: We tried to tell one of Your parables.

JESUS: Parables. Good. That's what I would have done. *(Andrew nods gratefully.)*

THOMAS: Which parable?

PHILIP: The Banquet.

ANDREW: You know, the one where the guests give excuses not to come, and then everyone else is invited.

JOHN: You chose THE BANQUET??

NATHANAEL: People get upset by that one!

JESUS: Of course they do.

ANDREW: Well, if it makes you feel any better, we first considered the Wheat and the Tares but thought better of it.

JESUS: I already told you some people wouldn't understand that parable.

THOMAS: I'm not even sure I understand the Wheat and the Tares.

JESUS: Give it time.

PHILIP: The problem is they did understand the parable and it caused a fight in the street.

ANDREW: Rioting. Between Jews and Gentiles.

PHILIP: Leander told us it gets worse every day. The prominent Hellenist priest changed his ways, which is good, but when he abdicated his duties as priest and leader, others wanted to fill the void, projects went undone, everyone got angry and started blaming each other …

ANDREW: And it led to stealing, actual fights in the streets, and many of the people are actually leaving their homes to wait out the violence.

BIG JAMES: That's the environment You suggest sending us into?!

JESUS (standing and moving about the room): What part of the parable caused this fight to break out?

PHILIP (exchanging a nervous look with Andrew): The people outside the city. The ones in the highways and hedges, the last to be invited and to accept the invitation.

JESUS (sighing): That's what I suspected.

JOHN: Speaking of which—the highways and hedges? Does that really refer to Gentiles?

JESUS: He who has ears to hear, let him hear. (a beat) We'll leave in the morning. Everyone, go home and gather your things. We take to the "highways and hedges" before dawn.

"[Jesus] said to them ... 'Truly, I say to you, if you have faith like a grain of mustard seed, you will say to this mountain, "Move from here to there," and it will move, and nothing will be impossible for you.'"

Matthew 17:20

Lesson 8

TRUST JESUS
all the time

EXT. DECAPOLIS COUNTRYSIDE

PHILIP: Rabbi, we didn't come here to cause trouble.

JESUS: It would appear trouble has found us.

BIG JAMES: So we should address it.

JESUS: And how do you propose to do that, Big James? My friends, sit with Me. We cannot go further until we agree on something.

(After an unsure beat, Big James, John, and Philip sit. Whispers and murmurs among the Gentile crowd looking on.)

JESUS (CONT'D) *(to the Gentiles)*: I am a rabbi, and as these Jewish brothers will tell you, we like to teach by asking questions, and we all like to solve problems by talking. It's even better if it starts with disagreement. So, feel free to listen, and if you'd like to argue a bit, that's fine too.

JUDAS *(regarding the growing factions around them with unease)*: Rabbi, we look weak and defenseless.

JESUS: On the way to Jairus's house in Capernaum, what happened when the woman, Veronica, touched Me?

ZEE: Power went out from You.

JESUS: No, I mean what happened to her?

THADDAEUS: She was healed.

JESUS: How?

ANDREW: By touching the fringe of Your garment.

JESUS: No. My friends, you forget so quickly. You are dear to Me, but your memories are short.

MATTHEW: You said, "Daughter, go in peace, your faith has made you well."

JESUS: Your what?

LITTLE JAMES: Faith.

THADDAEUS: Faith.

JESUS: Her faith. Many of you are afraid right now, instead of choosing to have faith in Me.

BIG JAMES: But, Rabbi, You must see what's happening all around us—

ANDREW: Of course He does, that's the point!

JUDAS: Rabbi, increase our faith!

JESUS: Judas … if you had faith the size of a grain of mustard seed, you could say to a mulberry tree, "Be uprooted and planted in the sea," and it would obey you.

MATTHEW: Can a mulberry tree grow in the sea?

THOMAS: He's making a point.

JESUS: Truly, if you have faith like a grain of mustard seed, you could say to a mountain, "Move from here to there," and it will move, and nothing will be impossible for you.

NATHANAEL: How? How do we get there?

PHILIP: Like Judas said, increase our faith!

JESUS: It's not about size, Philip. It's about who your faith is in. If you are secure in your faith in God, trusting in His promises, choosing His will for your life instead of your own … *(pinching His thumb and forefinger)* This sized faith is enough. The people we are ministering to … they are like bees, hovering among the flowers, waiting for them to open so they can sip the nectar and spread it to others. But they must see a faith in you that is secure, big or small.

Impossible Things

Trusting Jesus all the time sounds great but proved difficult for the twelve disciples when the crowds around them grew (Mark 3:7–10). And when people got angry (Mark 3:1–6). And hungry (Mark 6:31–44; 8:1–10, 14–21). And made accusations (Mark 7:1–5). Trusting was difficult for the twelve when they were asked to do things outside of their comfort zone, like travel to new places, preach to all kinds of people, and heal all kinds of ailments (Mark 6:7–13; 9:14–29). Trusting was difficult when storms raged and they felt neglected or even abandoned (Mark 4:35–41; 6:45–52). Trusting was difficult when they were confused or offended by something Jesus said or did (Mark 3:21; 8:31–38; 9:30–32; 10:13–16, 23–31). And trusting was difficult when Jesus allowed them to struggle.

Sound familiar?

Of course it does, because life is hard, and hard things challenge our faith. Hard things cause our trust in Jesus to waver and wane. But hard things also ultimately cause our faith to grow because God uses all things to work together for our good and for His glory (Rom. 8:28) and to make us more like Jesus (Rom. 8:29–30; 2 Pet. 1:3–4)—the author and perfecter of our faith (Heb. 12:2).

That's the promise of the narrow road that leads to life.

Through it, we'll be given ample opportunity to practice trusting the One we follow.

Your Turn

1. Name one or two things you're struggling to fully trust Jesus with.

Gotta Go Through

"We also boast in our sufferings, knowing that suffering
produces endurance, endurance produces character, and
character produces hope. Now this hope does not disappoint
us, because God's love has been poured out into our hearts
by the Holy Spirit, who has been given to us."

Romans 5:3–5 (ISV)

"Now listen, you rich people,
weep and wail because of the
misery that is coming on you. Your
wealth has rotted, and moths have
eaten your clothes. Your gold and
silver are corroded. Their corrosion
will testify against you and eat your
flesh like fire. You have hoarded
wealth in the last days. Look!
The wages you failed to pay the
workers who mowed your fields are
crying out against you. The cries
of the harvesters have reached
the ears of the Lord Almighty. You
have lived on earth in luxury and
self-indulgence. You have fattened
yourselves in the day of slaughter."

James 5:1–5 (NIV)

Yikes.

"Put not your trust in princes,
in a son of man, in whom there
is no salvation. When his breath
departs, he returns to the earth;
on that very day his plans perish."

Psalm 146:3–4

Hope that doesn't disappoint is
unique to Jesus. Meaning, there are lots of
things we place our hope and trust in that do, in fact,
disappoint. For example, money isn't all it's cracked
up to be. We spend our lives trying to get more of it,
believing our problems will be solved if or when we
do. But scan the celebrity horizon and you'll see how
not true that really is; Hollywood is a collective mess.
Broken relationships, addiction, abuse, and emptiness
abound.

Because money is a hope that disappoints.

What about relationship? Of course, some
people add to our lives in immeasurable ways and
obviously should be considered blessings from the
Lord. But no matter how wonderful a person may be,
when we place our hope and faith in other people,
we're inevitably going to be disappointed. We're all
imperfect, sinful, and limited. We're selfish, unaware,
and unable to be to each other what God intended
Himself to be for us.

Which means (human) relationship is a hope that disappoints.

What about success? After all, reaching a goal feels great and is something to be proud of. Problem is, when we place our hope in success, in titles, or in status, a lot of upkeep is required. Life is always moving and changing, and we feel the pressure to do more. But when we're looking for the affirmation that comes from accomplishment, no amount of it will suffice. Not permanently, anyway.

Because success is a hope that disappoints.

All that to say, the hope God cultivates deep in our hearts does *not* disappoint. But it's also hard won: first through Jesus's death and resurrection and then through our own.

We "die to self"—to our love of money, our desire to be accepted and validated by others, our drive to succeed—in order to live for Jesus. And then we transfer our hope to:

> "Do you not know that all of us who have been baptized into Christ Jesus were baptized into his death? We were buried therefore with him by baptism into death, in order that, just as Christ was raised from the dead by the glory of the Father, we too might walk in newness of life. For if we have been united with him in a death like his, we shall certainly be united with him in a resurrection like his. We know that our old self was crucified with him in order that the body of sin might be brought to nothing, so that we would no longer be enslaved to sin. For one who has died has been set free from sin. Now if we have died with Christ, we believe that we will also live with him. We know that Christ, being raised from the dead, will never die again; death no longer has dominion over him. For the death he died he died to sin, once for all, but the life he lives he lives to God. So you also must consider yourselves dead to sin and alive to God in Christ Jesus."
> Romans 6:3–11

a. What Jesus says about suffering:

"I have said these things to you, that in me you may have peace. In the world you will have tribulation. But take heart; I have overcome the world" (John 16:33).

b. Where Jesus says we're going:

"Let not your hearts be troubled. Believe in God; believe also in me. In my Father's house are many rooms. If it were not so, would I have told you that I go to prepare a place for you? And if I go and prepare a place for you, I will come again and will take you to myself, that where I am you may be also" (John 14:1–3).

c. Who Jesus says He is:

"I am the way, and the truth, and the life. No one comes to the Father except through me" (John 14:6).

He is our hope.

Your Turn

2. Other than Jesus, what or who do you tend to place your hope in?

3. The Bible promises that we'll have tribulation. The Bible also promises that God will use it to cultivate hope in our hearts. How might that change the way you suffer? How might that change the way you hope?

4. Explain how "dying to self" must be part of "entering through the narrow gate."

Culmination

"Therefore I tell you, do not be anxious about your life, what you will eat or what you will drink, nor about your body, what you will put on. Is not life more than food, and the body more than clothing? Look at the birds of the air: they neither sow nor reap nor gather into barns, and yet your heavenly Father feeds them. Are you not of more value than they? And which of you by being anxious can add a single hour to his span of life? And why are you anxious about clothing? Consider the lilies of the field, how they grow: they neither toil nor spin, yet I tell you, even Solomon in all his glory was not arrayed like one of these. But if God so clothes the grass of the field, which today is alive and tomorrow is thrown into the oven, will he not much more clothe you, O you of little faith? Therefore do not be anxious, saying, 'What shall we eat?' or 'What shall we drink?' or 'What shall we wear?' For the Gentiles seek after all these things, and your heavenly Father knows that you need them all. But seek first the kingdom of God and his righteousness, and all these things will be added to you. Therefore do not be anxious about tomorrow, for tomorrow will be anxious for itself. Sufficient for the day is its own trouble."

Matthew 6:25–34

For Bible Nerds (like us) Who Want to Know

"Dying to self": the continual denial of the sin nature in order to follow and trust Jesus every day, which means believers "die to self" on an ongoing basis.

Furthermore, at the moment of salvation, the Holy Spirit indwells believers, making obedience and Christlikeness possible. "Therefore, if anyone is in Christ, he is a new creation. The old has passed away; behold, the new has come" (2 Cor. 5:17).

"Enter through the narrow gate": Jesus is the gate that leads into God's kingdom. In order to be reconciled with God, and to spend eternity with Him in heaven, we must place our trust in Jesus's atoning death and miraculous resurrection.

"Jesus answered, 'I am the way and the truth and the life. No one comes to the Father except through me'" (John 14:6 NIV).

"The new has come": Isaiah mentions "the former things" several times (Isa. 41:22; 42:9; 43:9, 18; 46:9; 48:3; 65:17), but not with a sense of disdain. Our current culture teaches that *old* is bad and *new* is good. But in God's economy, the former things are foundational and helpful in the process of maturing and moving forward.

We see this principle at work when children grow *through* their childhood, not in spite of it; they are not to skip over the former things, nor are they to remain in them (1 Cor. 13:11–12).

In the same way, we are to "remember the former things of old" for their foundational value (Isa. 46:9), but we are to "remember not the former things" when it is time to move on to the new thing God is doing (Isa. 43:18–19).

See Matthew 14:13–21; Mark 6:32–44; Luke 9:10–17; John 6:1–15.

See Matthew 14:22–33; Mark 6:45–52; John 6:16–21.

"Have you not known? Have you not heard? The LORD is the everlasting God, the Creator of the ends of the earth. He does not faint or grow weary; his understanding is unsearchable. He gives power to the faint, and to him who has no might he increases strength. Even youths shall faint and be weary, and young men shall fall exhausted; but they who wait for the LORD shall renew their strength; they shall mount up with wings like eagles; they shall run and not be weary; they shall walk and not faint."
Isaiah 40:28–31

The final episode of season 3 of *The Chosen* brings together several plotlines and recounts two beloved New Testament stories: (1) the concern about food and Jesus's miraculous provision; and (2) the fear over safety and Jesus's miraculous, calming presence. Both mind-blowing experiences had the same impact on the hearts and minds of the disciples:

Jesus can be trusted.

And yet, anxiousness and fear remain a common part of our human experience. We know what Jesus did; we believe the stories. But still we struggle to believe He's the same yesterday, today, and forever (Heb. 13:8). We struggle to believe His promise to always provide (Matt. 6:25–34). We struggle to believe His promise to always be present (Matt. 28:20). We struggle to believe that His economy, His priorities, and His approval are literally all that matter (1 John 2:15–17).

We struggle.

But guess what?

God has made provision for that too:

"Therefore, since we are surrounded by so great a cloud of witnesses, let us also lay aside every weight, and sin which clings so closely, and let us run with endurance the race that is set before us, looking to Jesus, the founder and perfecter of our faith, who for the joy that was set before him

For Bible Nerds (like us) Who Want to Know

There are actually two miraculous feedings recorded in the Gospels (both near the Sea of Galilee): the feeding of the 5,000 in the countryside near Bethsaida (incidentally, this is the only miracle story told in all four Gospels—Matt. 14:13–21; Mark 6:32–44; Luke 9:10–17; John 6:1–15) and the feeding of the 4,000 in the Decapolis (Matt. 15:32–39; Mark 8:1–10).

Later in His ministry, Jesus actually referred to the two events together as He encouraged His followers to trust Him and to avoid the hypocrisy of people like the Pharisees (Matt. 16:5–12; Mark 8:14–21).

endured the cross, despising the shame, and is seated at the right hand of the throne of God" (Heb. 12:1–3).

Jesus is called the "founder and perfecter" of our faith—which means not only does He call us to Himself (He's the "founder" or "author" of our faith), He continues to lead, teach, correct, and form us (He's the "perfecter" of our faith). So, every day that we choose to follow Him, we become more like Him because He's faithful to make it so.

And as we follow, we'll see His provision and promises again and again.

The Old Testament Israelites were instructed to attach the *tzitzit* (tassels) to the four corners of their garments as reminders to obey the Lord's commands (Num. 15:37–41; Deut. 22:12).

We need reminders too, but sticky notes sometimes get knocked off easily and string tied around our fingers is annoying. Perhaps tassels on our clothing …

Your Turn

Let's get really specific here …

5. In light of your anxiousness and fear, what does it mean that Jesus is the same yesterday, today, and forever?

6. In light of your anxiousness and fear, what does it mean that Jesus will always provide and will always be present?

7. In light of your anxiousness and fear, what does it mean that God's economy, priorities, and approval are all that matter?

"Peace, Be Still"

> "And [Jesus] said to the sea, 'Peace! Be still!'
> And the wind ceased, and there was a great calm."
>
> Mark 4:39

It's not about the size of our faith. It never was, because trying harder to have bigger faith inevitably becomes akin to having faith in oneself. No—salvation through Jesus has only ever been about *Him* and His compassion, graciousness, power, and willingness to do what needs to be done to rescue and restore His creation.

Simply put, it's about Who your faith is in.

If you're secure in God, trusting in His promises, choosing His will for your life instead of your own, faith the size of a mustard seed will be enough to experience all that God has in store for you. He wants you to be a part of His kingdom building here on earth. He wants you to experience His peace that passes understanding and to rest in His presence. He wants you to know you're loved and to believe and act on His promises.

He wants you to enter through the narrow gate and walk beside Him, all the way to heaven.

Your Turn

8. Jesus's command for the wind and waves is the same one He has for you: Peace, be still.

How might you seek His peace, presence, and power today?

Prayer Focus

Praise Jesus because He controls the waves, including those in your life, whether ripples or tsunamis or something in between. Thank Him for being patient with you as you struggle to always trust Him. Ask Him to continue making you more like Him, and for opportunities to step out in faith. He will surely answer yes!

Sample Prayer

Dear Jesus,

Thank You for coming to earth, not only to die for my sins and rise again to secure my salvation, but also for living a perfect life. Your life displayed wisdom in the face of confusion, courage in the face of hardship, peace in the face of difficulty, and faithfulness in the face of despair. You understand the storms of life that I find myself in today, and I recognize that You're Lord of my storms. I do believe in You, but help my unbelief (Mark 9:24). Please make me more and more like You so that I can live in the midst of these storms with more of Your character (2 Pet. 1:3–12). When I need to step out in faith and take a stand for You, give me the wisdom, courage, peace, and faithfulness to do it with my hope set on You.

Amen.

EXT. SEA OF GALILEE

SIMON: John, keep rowing! What are you doing?

JOHN: Did anyone else just see that?

PHILIP: What?

JOHN: Over there!

(Everyone looks in the direction John is pointing. Nothing but darkness and waves.)

JUDAS: I don't see anything.

ZEE: What are we looking for?

(Lightning flashes again and there is the faintest apparition—a figure in the distance on the water.)

ANDREW (crying out in panic): A ghost! It's a ghost!

MATTHEW: A what??

BIG JAMES: It can't be.

ANDREW: We have to get out of here! Everyone row, row faster! Go!

SIMON (in a grave, calm voice): No! Nobody move.

ANDREW: Simon, what??

SIMON: I said everybody stop! Hold this position.

(Wild looks all around. Simon's gaze remains fixed on the exact last place where he saw the figure illuminated. Lightning strikes again, and we see the figure of Jesus among the waves. Simon's face remains rigid and unmoving among the flashes of lightning.)

ZEE: That's not a ghost.

ANDREW: Are you crazy?!

ZEE: Trust me. I know what a ghost looks like and that's not one.

JESUS: Do not be afraid, it's Me!

ANDREW: Jesus?!

PHILIP: How? What are You doing?!

BIG JAMES: Impossible!

THOMAS: How is this the second most incredible thing I've seen today?

JESUS: This surprises you? Did you learn nothing from today?

SIMON: If it is You, command me to come to You on the water.

ANDREW: Simon, no!

BIG JAMES: Are you out of your mind??

SIMON (pressing harder): If You are who You say You are, bid me to step out of this boat.

JESUS: You have faith to walk on this water?

SIMON: Absolutely! You can do whatever You command, and if You command the water to hold me, I will walk on it!

JESUS: If I call you to Me, you will step out in faith?

SIMON: Yes!

JESUS: Then why are you so upset?

SIMON: Why are You chasing after Gentiles when Your own people have problems right here! When Your own PERSON has problems? I've been right here in front of You, believing in You, and You're breaking up fights in the Decapolis!

(Another long pause as they stare at each other. At last—)

JESUS: Come to Me. You, weary and heavy-laden … I will give you rest.

(Simon rises. Takes off his sandals.)

ANDREW: Simon?!

(Amid murmurs and exclamations of fear, confusion, and excitement, Simon puts one hand on the edge of the boat. Jesus watches Simon's right leg slowly swing over the edge and inch its way down toward the water. Simon swings his left leg over and … stands, if unsteadily, on the water's surface. The disciples express nervous shock. Simon doesn't take his eyes off Jesus, who holds a hand to Simon.)

JESUS: Do you still have faith?

SIMON: Faith hasn't been my problem! I gave up everything to follow You, but You're healing total strangers!

JESUS: Why do you think I allow trials?

SIMON: I don't know!

JESUS: They prove the genuineness of your faith! They strengthen you! THIS is strengthening you! And Eden! Keep your eyes on Me!

(Waves crash into Simon. The disciples cry out, and Simon takes his eyes off Jesus. The waves are huge, merciless, and rolling. Everywhere he turns, the sea is scarier and fiercer. Fear takes over, and he starts to sink.)

SIMON: I'm sinking! Help!

(*The water is quickly up to Simon's chest.*)

SIMON: Lord, please! Save me!!

(*Jesus is moving toward him. The water is up to Simon's chin.*)

SIMON (CONT'D): Save me, I'm—

(*He goes under, his arm reaching out above the surface. Immediately, Jesus grips his forearm and Simon grips Jesus back. Jesus lifts him out of the water, shaking. Jesus looks into his eyes, full of sorrow. The two just stand, facing each other. Breathing and holding tightly. Finally, through a smile—*)

JESUS (*affectionately*): Oh you of a little faith. Why did you doubt?

(*Simon's eyes register shame and relief. He is surrendered.*)

SIMON: Please don't let me go. I'm sorry, I can't do this on my own, don't let me go, please.

JESUS: I have so much planned for you, Simon, including hard things—just keep your eyes on Me. I promise.

(*They step into the boat.*)

SIMON: Don't let me go.

JESUS (*turning to the raging sea*): Peace. Be still.

(*Jesus and Simon collapse against the mast. Simon still grips Jesus, repeating—*)

SIMON: Don't let me go. Please. Don't let me go.

(*The peaceful waters gently lap against the hull, and all the disciples are soaked, exhausted, and spellbound. For Simon, no one else exists in the world but Jesus. He weeps softly as Jesus strokes his wet hair.*)

JESUS: I'm here … I'm always here. I let people get hungry … but I feed them.

SIMON: Don't let me go. Don't let me go. Don't let me go.

"Enter by the narrow gate. For the gate is wide and the way is easy that leads to destruction, and those who enter by it are many. For the gate is narrow and the way is hard that leads to life, and those who find it are few."

Matthew 7:13-14

CONCLUSION

Those who find the way to life are few.

Why is that?

Because it's hard. And the truth is, we sinful humans prefer easy. But, oh, that we'd choose Jesus anyway! There is, in fact, beauty and peace and joy and hope and rest through the narrow gate—God never disappoints.

Of course, life disappoints. Sin broke the world God made, and we live under its consequences. Making matters worse, the shifting sand of the wide road ensures our destruction and eternal separation from the God who loves us, the One who entered into our brokenness and became both our sacrificial Lamb and our Cornerstone—the Rock of our salvation and the start of the world's restoration.

> "And he came and preached
> peace to you who were far off and
> peace to those who were near. For
> through him we both have access

Sacrificial Lamb:
In OT days, perfect, spotless lambs were sacrificed to God for the atonement of sin (Ex. 12:5, Lev. 4:32).

Because Jesus lived a perfect life without sin, His death on the cross became the perfect and permanent sacrifice of atonement for any and all who choose to believe in Him (Heb. 9:11–14; 1 Pet. 1:9; John 1:29, 36).

Cornerstone:
the first stone placed in the foundation of a structure, and the reference point for where all other stones are placed.

Scripture makes several comments about Jesus being the ultimate cornerstone and reference for life (Isa. 28:16–17; Ps. 118:19–23; Matt. 21:42; Acts 4:11–12; Eph. 2:20; 1 Pet. 2:4–10).

in one Spirit to the Father. So then you are no longer strangers and
aliens, but you are fellow citizens with the saints and members of the
household of God, built on the foundation of the apostles and prophets,
Christ Jesus himself being the cornerstone, in whom the whole
structure, being joined together, grows into a holy temple in the Lord."
Ephesians 2:17–21

Solid ground is available to us through Jesus. Because of His victory over death, we're raised to life with Him (Rom. 6:6–11) and reconciled to the Father (Rom. 5:8–11) and indwelled by the Spirit (Rom. 8:9–11)—which enables us to *continue* following Jesus all the way to heaven where the perfection of Eden will be restored.

Which means the way of the Chosen is Jesus Himself.

He is the narrow gate that leads to LIFE.

Revelation 22:1–5

"Then the angel showed me

the river of the water of life,

bright as crystal, flowing from the throne

of God and of the Lamb through

the middle of the street of the city; also,

on either side of the river, the tree of life with its

twelve kinds of fruit, yielding its fruit each month.

The leaves of the tree were for the healing of the

nations. No longer will there be anything accursed,

but the throne of God and of the Lamb will be in it,

and his servants will worship him. They will see

his face, and his name will be on their foreheads.

And night will be no more.

They will need no light of lamp or sun, for the

Lord God

will be their light, and they will reign forever and ever."

NOTES

NOTES

NOTES

NOTES

NOTES

NOTES

NOTES

NOTES

NOTES

ABOUT THE AUTHORS

Amanda Jenkins is an author, speaker, and mother of four. She is the lead creator for *The Chosen*'s extra content, including *The Chosen* devotionals, volumes I, II, and III, and *The Chosen* children's books *Jesus Loves the Little Children* and *The Shepherd*. She lives in Texas with her kids and husband, Dallas, creator of *The Chosen*.

Dallas Jenkins is a filmmaker, author, and speaker. Over the past twenty years, he has directed and produced over a dozen films for companies such as Warner Brothers, Lionsgate, Universal Studios, and Hallmark Channel. He is now the creator of The Chosen, the first-ever multi-season show about the life of Christ and the highest crowd-funded media project of all-time. He lives with his family in Texas where they now film the show.

The official evangelical biblical consultant for *The Chosen* TV series, **Douglas S. Huffman** (PhD, Trinity Evangelical Divinity School) is Professor of New Testament and Associate Dean of Biblical and Theological Studies at Talbot School of Theology (Biola University) in California. Specializing in New Testament Greek, Luke–Acts, and Christian Thought, he is the author of *Verbal Aspect Theory and the Prohibitions in the Greek New Testament* and *The Handy Guide to New Testament Greek*; contributing editor of such books as *God Under Fire: Modern Scholarship Reinvents God, How Then Should We Choose? Three Views on God's Will and Decision Making*, and *Christian Contours: How a Biblical Worldview Shapes the Mind and Heart*; and contributor to several theological journals and reference works. Dr. Huffman can be seen on *The Chosen*'s "Bible Roundtables" on *The Chosen* app. He enjoys working with Biola undergraduate students, pointing them to Scripture as God's Word for us today.